Praise for *The Natural Navigator*

"*THE NATURAL NAVIGATOR* is a wonderfully stimulating book. Tristan Gooley sidesteps technology to celebrate our own powers of observation, and suggests that the art of natural navigation is something we should never have forgotten." —**MICHAEL PALIN**

"THIS WONDERFUL BOOK takes the skill set back several generations . . . to the vanishing (but often surprisingly simple) arts of navigating by sun, moon, starts, and natural phenomena. . . . A must for any lover of the outdoors." —**TIM JEPSON**, *The Telegraph*

"GOOLEY IS A fine writer with a philosophical passion for the subject, and he occasionally veers into areas that are perhaps not strictly within the remit of the book, but these are effortlessly pleasant diversions that add to the whole. His timing is strong, with anecdotes dropped in just at the right intervals to keep you turning the pages. His advice is at times glorious in its simplicity and fascinating in its execution." —**LAURENCE MACKIN**, *The Irish Times*

"A DEFINITIVE VOLUME on the subject."—**PAUL GELDER**, *Yachting Monthly*

"IN A SAT-NAV dominated world, where GPS and a host of other acronyms designed to get us from A to B have overtaken paper maps, it is refreshing to meet someone who understands technology, but prefers to find his way by practicing the rare and ancient art of using nature's signposts, from puddle patterns to shadow length. . . . I'm hooked." —**PAUL EVANS**, *BBC Wildlife Magazine*

"As GOOLEY REMINDS us, navigation is, first of all, about understanding where you are. His marvelous book is a good starting point." —**MICK MERRON**, *Geographical Magazine*

"GOOLEY'S CALM, CONTEMPLATIVE authority on matters solar, lunar, and celestial establishes his guru credentials—but it's his revelations about the clues that lie scattered about the natural environment that really entrance: how puddles drying on paths, the shapes of sand dunes, the graininess of scree on the lee of a slope can all be enlisted to summon compass points to your horizon." —**CHRIS BORN**, *Time Out London*

THE EXPERIMENT BECAUSE EVERY BOOK IS A TEST OF NEW IDEAS

The
Natural
Navigator

Tristan Gooley

A Watchful Explorer's Guide to a Nearly Forgotten Skill

THE EXPERIMENT
NEW YORK

THE NATURAL NAVIGATOR: *A Watchful Explorer's Guide to a Nearly Forgotten Skill*

Copyright © Tristan Gooley, 2010, 2011
Illustration on page 100 © Science Museum/SSPL
Illustration on page 169 © Ocean Planet/Smithsonian
All other illustrations © Ruth Murray

The Experiment, LLC
260 Fifth Avenue
New York, NY 10001-6425
www.theexperimentpublishing.com

The Natural Navigator was first published in the United Kingdom by Virgin Books, an imprint of Ebury Publishing, a Random House Group Company. This first revised North American edition is published by arrangement with Random House.

Excerpts from *Zen and the Art of Motorcycle Maintenance* by Robert Pirsig, published by Bodley Head, reprinted by the permission of the Random House Group Ltd. Excerpts from *The Worst Journey in the World* by Apsley Cherry-Garrard appear by permission of the Scott Polar Research Institute, University of Cambridge.

The Experiment's books are available at special discounts when purchased in bulk for premiums and sales promotions as well as for fundraising or educational use. For details, contact us at info@theexperimentpublishing.com.

Library of Congress Control Number: 2010934221
ISBN 978-1-61519-029-4

Cover design by Davvi | davvi.com
Cover photo © Steve Gottlieb/Stock Connection
Text design by Lindsay Nash

Manufactured in the United States of America
First printing January 2011

10 9 8 7 6 5 4 3 2 1

For Sophie, Benedict, and Vincent

Contents

PROLOGUE
Two Journeys

The idea for this book came many years ago and stemmed from a desire to launch a salvage operation. A fundamental human skill was disappearing, as efficient and ubiquitous technology came to dominate our understanding of what it means to find our way. I dreamed of creating a record of the skills of natural navigation, lest they be forgotten altogether. The idea evolved dramatically over the years, as I came to realize that not only was the rare art of natural navigation in danger of extinction, but that the modern world had misunderstood its potential entirely. Nobody seemed to regard what were once practical tools for survival as a contemporary art, but that is how I see it. An art, and one that is at its most beautiful and powerful when it is treated as exactly that, as something exquisite and profound, not a chapter of history or a series of tricks for the modern survivalist.

When I was ten we went on our summer holiday to Bembridge, on the Isle of Wight. At the end of a five-day dinghy sailing course, the instructor approached my sailing partner and me as we prepared our little wooden dinghy for the water.

"Where would you like to go today?"

The three of us discussed some options, casually, as though this was the most normal thing and then my sailing partner and I launched our Mirror dinghy and set sail. We were going for a picnic on the neighboring beach. I can remember sitting in that boat as we made our own way through the high seas of our imagination (the safety boat was tactfully out of sight). I was only ten years old, and somehow I had garnered the skills to go wherever I wanted. Not where my teachers told me to go, not where my parents wanted me to go, but where I wanted to go. Heady thoughts indeed.

The journeys grew a little more ambitious over time and by my mid-twenties I had some basic experience of trekking, sailing, and flying a light aircraft. It was not the physical activities that were holding my interest, but the science and art behind the ability to go places—the skills that were allowing me to understand and shape journeys. This art had a name, I discovered: It was "navigation."

As part of a desire to pursue my interest in this wonderful art, I decided to try to fly solo and then sail single-handed across the Atlantic. Seven very full years later (during which time I became a father twice over, and my work pressures sky-rocketed) I achieved this on January 1, 2008, and was presented by the Duke of Edinburgh with the Royal Institute of Navigation's Award at the Royal Geographical Society.

This book is about a different journey, one that had taken place in the shadow of my more visible Atlantic excursions. It is also the more interesting journey.

In the midst of studying books at night about air law and learning how to find my way using radios, I came to the awkward realization that the technical detail that was the stuff of my studies had little in common with a passion that had been within me since early childhood. It was an uncomfortable feeling, one that frustrated me. I loved going places—creating and experiencing journeys—long before I understood that the word "navigation" could unite my disparate interests. But it was the sense of connection that the journeys brought that really excited me, the contact with the world around me. I began to read as widely as possible on the subject of instrument-free navigation. My sense of frustration lifted as an alternative interest developed strongly alongside a conventional one.

In a bid to gain the skills to undertake the journeys I dreamed of, I had been forced into another world, one as removed from my romantic impulses as can be imagined. A world of screens and bureaucracy, of checklists and never-ending acronyms. Over the years I became familiar with not only GPS but also AIS, ILS, ADF, NDB, VHF, DME, UHF, SSB, VOR, ASI, VSI . . . the list seems to run on indefinitely. It was clear that this was a world I needed to understand, but not one in which I wanted to live. My future lay in understanding the natural side of journeys.

There was a sense of mounting exhilaration as I began to immerse myself in the subject of natural navigation. The world that around me came more alive than ever with the question, "Which way am I looking?" It acted as the key that could unlock the natural world. I quickly came to realize that it is not the answer that is all-important, but how we arrive at it, or even fail to arrive at it. For that reason, this book will attempt to do more than answer the question, "Which way am I looking?"

There is a difference between finding direction and *knowing* direction. It is possible to teach someone a method of finding direction, accurately to within 1 degree, in under five minutes. They would have the practical knowledge to undertake a simple journey without a map, compass, or GPS, but that is all. They may have found direction, but they would remain disconnected from their environment.

The following chapters demonstrate how it is possible to find your way using natural navigation, but my primary aim is to give an insight into the beauty and possibilities of the subject. Natural navigation can be as much a mental journey as a physical one, and it is this that makes it a profound art.

The way we use our senses and mind to answer the question, "Which way am I looking?" can lead to thoughts, connections, and ideas that are as exciting as any journey that follows. You are about to catapult yourself into the top 1 percent of natural navigators in the world. Welcome to a very rare art indeed.

Tristan Gooley

INTRODUCTION
The Art of Natural Navigation

When analytic thought, the knife, is applied to experience, something is always killed in the process. That is fairly well understood, at least in the arts. Mark Twain's experience comes to mind, in which, after he had mastered the analytic knowledge needed to pilot the Mississippi River, he discovered the river had lost its beauty. Something is always killed. But what is less noticed in the arts—something is always created too.

—Robert M. Pirsig,
Zen and the Art of Motorcycle Maintenance

Natural navigation is the art of finding your way by using nature. It consists mainly of the rare skill of being able to determine direction without the aid of tools or instruments and only by reference to natural clues including the sun, the moon, the stars, the land, the sea, the weather, the plants, and the animals. It is about observation and deduction.

Natural navigation is an ancient art, borne from an era when there were no alternatives. Any attempt to fully understand it must begin by looking back. The earliest journeys hold many mysteries. We know that they took place, since human beings found their way to every far corner of the globe, but there is very little physical evidence of them. Archaeological evidence can trace the routes but gives little insight into the earliest methods of navigating. A 13,000-year-old human femur has been discovered on an island off the Pacific coast of the United States that was separate from the mainland at the time of its owner's life. This makes it clear that humans were attempting boat journeys at the time, but does not begin to explain how they were finding their way.

Natural selection dictated that those animals and humans unable to work out a way of getting to where they needed to be in order to survive did not contribute to the next generation's gene pool. If the outward journey was not always critical, the return one was. There is no harm in going for a wander, but if the ability to return to food and shelter was missing, then that adventure may have proved fatal. Evolutionary theory tends to focus on the physical: as a general rule, the faster the animal, the better its chances. However, in the race for survival (as in all other journeys) speed in the wrong direction was a fast way to lose out. We now know that we exist in part because our ancestors learned how to navigate, even if we do not yet fully understand how they did so.

Ancient journeys can enrich contemporary ones, because the ancients learned to read their surroundings more skillfully than most modern travelers can. They have much to teach, but it is not laid out in ancient textbooks. Some of the pieces of the puzzle come from oral traditions or even the very earliest images etched in stone.

The myths of a particular culture connected its people with their surroundings, their past, and each other. Myths should never be totally discounted, because even if a story is not meant to be understood literally, the teller still must add a degree of authenticity in order to convince the audience. One way of ensuring this was by making the context in which the story was set as detailed and accurate as possible. The narrative of myths may be fantastical, but they are set in the world of their audience. The ancient Egyptian god Horus may not help us to navigate directly, but the myths that surround him illuminate the way in which the ancient Egyptians perceived the sky. Horus took the form of a falcon, and his two eyes were the sun and moon. He had injured his left eye, the moon, and was sometimes blind in it, but even when he could see it was always weaker than his right eye, the sun. This helps demonstrate the Egyptian familiarity with the moon's phases as it moved from an invisible new moon to a full moon. The sun has no such phases.

Myths were not conceived to assist the modern traveler, so the lessons in them are often hidden. Tales about characters like Perseus might seem to offer little to the contemporary navigator, but knowing that he rescued Andromeda from a sea monster can help make sense of the night sky—the constellations of Perseus and Andromeda are neighbors.

Religious texts are another ancient source. They exist either as a reflection of reality or an attempt to explain it, depending on your viewpoint, but either way they yield valuable information about early journeys, perspectives, and methods. The Koran refers to the use of rivers, the sun, moon, stars, landmarks, and shadows as means of navigating and even points readers to them: "Surely in this there are signs for men of understanding."

The history of human navigation is mostly concerned with an attempt to answer the question, "How did people find their way?", but a better place to start might be to ask, "Why?" Any motive for navigating is inseparable from our motives for travel in general, as navigation is one of the practical faces of travel.

Why Navigate at All?

The legendary Viking Erik the Red fled Norway with his parents in the tenth century following a murder and survived a crossing of the cold North Atlantic to Iceland. Unfortunately he was blamed for some violent deaths there, too, and so he moved on again, this time to Greenland. The name "Greenland" was chosen by Erik to entice the Icelanders to come to a land that was anything but green. Twenty-five ships set sail from Iceland to follow Erik to the new land. Eleven of them didn't make it there to discover just how optimistic the name Greenland was, but a colony was established. Nonetheless, Erik the Red is credited with opening up that land and the sea route to Europeans.

Violence on a grander scale than Erik's has been a motive both for great journeys and pioneering navigation. War and conquest have spurred nations on to epic undertakings. The hunger for new territory can be found behind many of the great expeditions, from the ancient Egyptian ruler Necho II (probably the pharaoh referred to in several books of the Bible), who wanted to see canals forced through land and sent ships to circumnavigate Africa, and on down to the European scramble for colonies in the late nineteenth century. The earliest journeys were probably often triggered by hunger and the struggle for survival. When the resources of a land fail, the choice for the starving population is to move or die where they stand. But the human story is one of an appetite that is hard to satisfy. One navigator might assist in the fight against hunger as she straps a chart to her thigh pad, climbs aboard a Hercules transport aircraft, and prepares to fly food aid into the Sudan. Another navigator tries to satisfy a different hunger by poring over the chart on the bridge of a container ship in the Chinese port of Ningbo, preparing to set out with a cargo of plastic toys bound for the United States.

One of our many modern conceits is to believe that the desire to travel to satisfy intellectual curiosity belongs to our era, but how erroneous this is. The ancient Greek Solon traveled to Egypt on a sightseeing trip, while the Roman poet Manilius wrote of his astonishment that people would travel to see art and temples rather than to stand and wonder at the volcano of Mt Etna.

Not every journey has a grand purpose. Rather, there is a strong human tradition of impetuousness, spontaneity, and adventure. The great natural navigators of the Micronesian island of Puluwat have long had a habit of getting drunk and then sailing to the neighboring island of Pikelot:

> A minimum of equipment and any available food is loaded
> aboard and they depart, singing and shouting as they work
> their way across the lagoon and out of the pass, while their
> wives and other sober souls scowl their disapproval on shore.

Part of the motive for these sorts of journeys may be a temporary flight from responsibility. Who can honestly claim to have never wished to pack a bag and "get away from it all?"

Some desires are best admitted to even if they do not feature as openly around dinner tables as they might. For instance, that we travel for sex. Long before the Pacific explorers of the eighteenth century returned with tales of the beauty of the women and their generosity with their sexual favors, new lands have hinted at the possibility of sexual adventure. There is inevitably a phallocentric bias to our historical understanding in this area, but it has never been wholly one-sided. Inanna, the Sumerian goddess of sexual love, looked at her vulva and, being delighted with the power of her genitals, set out in a boat on a mission of sexual predation. She got the god Enki drunk, exhausted him, and made off with a boat full of the prizes she sought. This was not the last time such tactics have proved effective.

We travel not only to escape, consume, and copulate but also to think and create. "When I stay in one place I can hardly think at all," wrote Jean-Jacques Rousseau.

Navigation is one aspect of travel, but our chances of getting the most from it are greatly increased if we question our reasons for each journey. Whether we are moved by hunger, thirst, greed, love, sex, war, philosophy, culture, or a desire to smell the sea, our motives will likely determine how much there is to be gained by looking at the world in a different way.

The Silent Revolution

Navigation has undergone a metamorphosis. There has been a silent, technical revolution in wayfaring.

Simple instruments like the kamal, a wooden card and length of string that helped to measure angles, began to appear a little over a thousand years ago. The kamal was the forerunner of the sextant, which does no more than measure angles quite accurately. One of the earliest glimpses of the compass can be found in a French poem by Guy de Provins at the start of the thirteenth century. And so we witness the start of the process whereby an individual with previously valuable knowledge of the stars, the sun, the moon, and the sea itself is to be usurped by an "ugly brown stone" to which iron sticks. And now the compass itself is having its supremacy tested by the irrepressible rise of satellite navigation.

The history of the development of navigational instruments has been tackled elsewhere, and there is no need to dwell on it here. But an understanding of the seismic change in the relationship between the navigator and the natural world that has occurred with the development of increasingly sophisticated instruments is helpful when studying the role of navigation in a journey.

The impact of this revolution is given perspective by looking at the changing role of the navigator in society. The relationship between the navigator and their community reveals much about that society's relationship with the natural world. In many societies there are cultural links between maturity and an ability to navigate. Young Australian Aboriginal men are expected to set out on a journey of some length as part of the rite of passage to adulthood. The acquisition of navigation skills is seen as a metaphor for the gaining of life skills and is marked in this ritualistic way.

In the Pacific, navigators were traditionally afforded an elevated status in the social hierarchy, not far below that of a priest. Their knowledge was passed down from father to son and jealously guarded. In a similar spirit to the notion of the one-eyed man being king in the land of the blind, pioneering navigators were probably able to choose their role, since they were the people who could enable journeys and sometimes made new settlements possible. There is the legend of Nana-Ula, who led a huge expedition 1,000 years ago from Tahiti to Hawaii and later became the first king of Hawaii.

It is not surprising that in places like the Arctic, where life is fragile and nature harsh, any skills that improve the odds of survival hold an important place in the society. For the Inuit, "A good navigator is quietly revered, a poor one gently ridiculed."

In our industrialized society, the navigator is in danger of losing the place afforded to those with valuable skills and becoming viewed as just one more machine operator. The job often disappears altogether as the task of navigating by computer is assimilated into a broader job: There are still pilots in the cockpits of aircraft who navigate effectively, but very few "navigators" left in these cockpits.

Why Navigate Naturally?

Natural navigation is one of the rarest arts on the planet, but it has not yet disappeared altogether. We tend to see it primarily in relation to our understanding of how earlier cultures looked at the world around them. There is something patronizing in the modern attitude to the way things were done in the past. It is common to encounter the notion that the degree to which the ancients were connected to the natural world indicates their lack of sophistication. This attitude reflects a peculiar modern illness. We consider our need to lead lives that leave no time for contemplation of our physical environment as superior, but in doing so we often fail to recognize what has been lost. The historical treatment of the subject of natural navigation helps the modern-day navigator to understand what is possible, but it is not where the subject should be confined. Natural navigation does not belong in a museum.

The second way in which natural navigation has endured is as a survival technique. There are very few books on the subject of natural navigation itself, but it surfaces in a superficial way as a few pages in the hundreds of books that cover survival skills. The approach in this context is nearly always ruthlessly pragmatic, for good reasons. The sun or stars are used to find direction, but any deeper understanding is not a priority. Survival is by definition a desperate and urgent business. By necessity this approach strips out almost all that is fascinating in the subject. Survivalists are not going to spend time contemplating the ancient Greek astronomer Hipparchus or any arcane relationship that might exist between beaches and the moon.

However, the biggest drawback to the survival philosophy is that it is not relevant to most outdoor experiences. For every situation in which survival is at stake, there must be more than a million journeys of varying types in which the participants can enrich their experience of the outdoors through a greater understanding of nature.

Sometimes the subject is taught as a series of "tricks," but looking at direction in relation to nature in this perfunctory way can rob us of the opportunity of connecting properly with it. There is a subtle difference between finding direction and knowing direction—it is sometimes possible to find direction using nature in seconds without feeling any great understanding of the natural world. To get to *know* direction it is necessary to have a more fundamental understanding of the world we move through. If the aim is to enrich an experience, then it is more important to understand why the methods work than to be able to use them. This is the defining difference between survival navigation and natural navigation.

Necessity is the force that shaped navigation methods, and for thousands of years the greatest need was improved safety. Navigation has always been connected to safety. We may conclude that safety remains the top priority in any journey, but we should not lose sight of the reasons for each journey. The aim might only be to reach the destination safely, or it might be to enjoy the challenge of finding it.

There is an old joke about how most of us drive clapped-out, uncomfortable bangers all our lives, but then those very few who "make it" go out and buy a bespoke Rolls-Royce—only to hand the keys to someone else to enjoy the drive. Why, when the fun in a journey can be in understanding the world we move through, would we want to hand that all over to a GPS unit?

The best news is that it does not have to be a choice between safety and experience. It is now possible get the best of both worlds. Natural navigators can use nature to find our way without diminishing safety at all, and, if used responsibly, nature actually enhances safety.

There is a beautiful irony in all of this. The new technologies actually enable us to reconnect with nature in a way that might not have been possible 100 years ago. The fact that we now have navigation instruments to hand can provide us with the opportunity to take more notice of the navigational clues that nature offers. The land or sea, the sky, the feel of wind on our face can be given more attention without leaving the instruments at home.

A very common question is whether being able to navigate naturally is a necessary skill. Since it is quite possible to get through our daily lives without any knowledge of this most ancient of arts, the answer must be "no." However, it is also true that we can get by in life without any knowledge of music, art, drama, or history. So a better answer to this question is perhaps that it does not matter if you are walking to the coffee shop or sailing across an ocean, natural navigation can provide a unique insight into the world around you.

Natural navigation is a skill for the present and future, not the past. It is an art for when things are going well much more than when our lives are in danger. For many, it becomes a "key to unlocking a fascinating text in the Earth's rich library."

Getting Ready

Familiarity is the foundation stone of all early navigation experiences. Very young children like to keep parents or home within sight and take comfort from recognizing clues to help them to find their way. As the child grows older, the distance from their comfort zone of home and parent to which they are prepared and able to travel grows steadily.

By the time of adulthood the process is so intrinsic that little thought is given to understand "how" it works. From a familiarity with surroundings, a series of associations develop, most of which are logical and useful: Living on top of a hill will quickly lead to the realization that a downhill path is unlikely to be the route home. But humans are also prone to making incorrect assumptions: We may, for example, conclude that a town is in the direction of some buildings we can see in the distance, whereas in fact it is in the opposite direction. Natural navigation is therefore about effectively combining observation and deduction. Finding a clue to direction is no good if it leads to the wrong conclusion.

We all learn to "read" our home areas as a series of recognizable landmarks, man-made ones like shops and road junctions to broader natural clues like where we are in relation to a river. There does not appear to be any bias toward either natural or manmade landmarks, only toward what works. We tend to shift our attention automatically to what seems to us to be the most effective clue, sometimes to the detriment of our understanding of previous ones. Some have attributed the loss of native navigational methods in North Alaska to the arrival of artificial but very effective landmarks like radio masts, towers, and other tall buildings. This point was demonstrated when in 1990 the authorities tried to take down some large radar installations. The local Inuit people asked that they be left standing as they were useful landmarks, visible from forty miles away. This adaptability can also be seen in the animal kingdom: Bees look for patterns that they recognize, regardless of whether they are natural or man-made.

Here, then, is the first system for wayfaring without instruments. All we need to do is become familiar with the landmarks of an area and then remember where they are, relative to each other and our destination. There are only two real flaws to this method, one of which you will probably have spotted already. Landmark navigation only works on land and only if you are already very familiar with an area. The second flaw is that our perception of the world around us is subjective. We each develop a unique memory map of an area, which will vary significantly from that of any other person. Think how many times someone has given you directions in their local area that they seem to think are idiot proof: ". . . go over the hill, turn left at the pine trees and then it's second right after the house with the red roof . . ." Was that undulation back there the hill, or is the hill still ahead? Are those the trees they meant and is that roof red or orange?

There is a way of describing locations that does not require familiarity and is not subjective, but a new way of describing places is needed to use it. In fact, it is a new language.

Taming Conventions

Every location in the world can be described in terms of its direction from a known point and the distance from that point. In order for this to work both parties must understand exactly where that known point is, how to describe direction, and what the chosen unit of distance means. Once those criteria have been met, there are no rights or wrongs, only what works. The international navigational language that has become most prevalent is to describe location by referring how far north or south a place is from the equator (latitude) and how far east or west it is from Greenwich, London (longitude). Direction is described by cutting the circle of all possible directions up into 360 degrees, starting at the direction of the "north," which means "toward the North Pole," and working clockwise all the way back round to it. This is the most widespread way of describing place and direction, but it is not a universal system. Many Muslims understand direction relative to Mecca, and many people think more locally, hence expressions like "I'm heading up to town" might easily mean heading south, not north.

The use of "degrees" is a common and useful convention, but one that can make a natural situation appear cold and mathematical. Degrees are normally measured by instruments, something we will not be doing at all, but the concept remains a natural one: 10 degrees is simply one thirty-sixth of a circle, whether it is measured by a sextant, compass, or an outstretched fist. An outstretched fist is a rough measure of 10 degrees for most people, since we share similar body proportions.

The conventions over distance are more convoluted, since the means by which distance is measured differs between nations to this day. But here, too, we find roots in nature. The "mile" stems from the Roman term "*mille passus*," denoting 1,000 paces, and the meter was defined by the French in 1791 as one ten-millionth of the distance from the North Pole to the equator, via Paris.

All of this just amounts to a language, a kind of shorthand for communicating directions and distances. There is nothing that makes any one method of shorthand inherently more correct than another. If you find it easier to discuss direction among friends in terms relative to a local landmark and to communicate distance using fruit, then not even the Royal Institute of Navigation can call that wrong. Birmingham is still in the same place if it is described as being 947,976 banana lengths in the direction of The Hound and Fox from the post office as if it is described as being 100 miles northwest of London, or 52.5 degrees north of the equator and nearly 2 degrees west of Greenwich. The truth is that most people find the latter two methods more meaningful, which is how conventions become established. The conventions are only a language that is meant to make life easier, but learning a new language is often daunting and can make navigation seem foreign, even when a lot of the concepts are natural and simple. The same is true of other areas where conventions have grown up, like astronomy.

Memorizing the names of stars does not make them any more beautiful. Constellations do not exist except in our imagination, so it is an entirely personal decision whether we adopt the conventional names or give them our own ones. Take the star Castor in the constellation Gemini. Is it just that, a star in a constellation? Or is it the mortal son of Tyndareus, brother of Helen of Troy? Is it a sextuple star system that is fifty-two light-years from Earth? Perhaps it is a "beaver," since this is what "castor" means in both Greek and Latin? Of course it is all of these things and many more, depending on the viewpoint we choose.

As with so many human skills, the art of navigation has become arcane through convention, which is a shame. It is a wonderful subject, and one that is so very relevant to our lives. It would be so much more accessible and therefore, probably, popular if it were not so shrouded in technical language. Most of what is popularly described as "exploration" these days has more in common with navigation than exploration. Exploration captures the imagination of so many because it is seen through powerful images and gripping narratives, but the art that makes these adventures possible is navigation.

Wherever I have used the established conventions in this book, it is because they stand the best chance of being meaningful, not because they represent the beauty in the subject. Natural navigators should feel free to translate these conventions into the language they find most comfortable—bananas or anything else.

The first stage in becoming a natural navigator is to master observation, and the first lesson in this area is that observation is not all about the eyes. And even when it is about the eyes, there is more to it than meets our eyes.

A Sense of Connection

The natural world is a dull place. Another furry creature appears before us on TV as the monotone drawl of a commentator waxes all over it. A boat moves lazily through endless blue water beneath a hot bland sun, and the crew play cards and sweat tedium. Homogenous trees fly past a car window. And then, in an instant, everything changes.

The air squeezing in through the thin gap in the car window brings with it the unmistakeable scent of the sea; we are approaching the coast, memories of childhood car trips flood our minds, and nostalgia pushes us to gaze out through the window. We grasp at memories of chewing sand in sandwiches as our eyes meet those of a deer for a second. It holds our stare and then flees.

There is another splash; it comes from the bow of the boat, but is different from the other watery sounds and so we race forward with the rest of the crew and find a porpoise playing off the bow wave. As we step back we notice the albatross circling high above the boat and someone warns us that we will suffer the torment of the Ancient Mariner if we do not respect the bird.

Our fingers reach for the remote control as we spot a strange shape on the leggy spider, red emblem, an hourglass. We recognize the shape and pause before switching channels, long enough for the commentator's voice to come to life as he growls excitably about the black widow, its venom that can paralyze and suffocate us. He continues, explaining the female's habit of killing and eating her partner after mating. The synapses fire. Our imagination goes to work. The natural world has ceased to be a dull place.

The pressure on our time leads us to compartmentalize the things we observe in the world around us, but this habit cuts us off from the richness of detail in our surroundings. It makes us less aware.

Learning to navigate naturally forces us to reexamine the ways we connect to our physical environment, how our senses are pivotal to effective natural navigation and how they in turn define our experience and understanding. Sensual awareness is critical to finding our way without instruments, but it is also important if we do not want to be denied some of the texture of a journey.

Over time, the natural navigator comes to use the senses intuitively. American explorer and sea captain Edmund Fanning awoke suddenly in the middle of the Pacific, in the middle of the night, rushed on deck, and ordered his crew to heave-to. It was not until the following morning that they realized this had saved them from a reef less than a mile away. Fanning had felt the proximity of the reef through the action of the water.

It is easy for those of us who are not blind or partially sighted to take the sense of sight for granted. Our eyes feed far more detailed information to our brains than we can possibly process and so a filtration takes place. Our brain sorts through the visual information, tries to make sense of it, and allows us to focus on what seems most important. This has been honed by evolution: Our brain and eyes will work quickly together to spot and identify a prowling tiger before spending time to analyze the colors of a flower. It is efficient, but it is not perfect for two key reasons. The first is that there are biases in our view of the world, often psychological, and probably driven by evolutionary necessity. These biases manifest themselves in what we notice. We are much more sensitive to shape than we are to color, for example. We will notice the path curving away in front of us, but fail to spot the subtle shift in hue from one side to the other.

The second reason is that we are no longer primarily concerned with survival and so it is often necessary to unlearn our instinctive response to the world we see—we don't need to focus only on perceived threats. The modern natural navigator must stop, look and think about the environment in a way that even our most naturally astute ancestors may not have done. Very little of nature is entirely random, but it can appear complex and chaotic, and so the challenge is to study this complexity and look for patterns that provide clues.

This need not be an arduous process and once accustomed to looking for detail it is a habit that yields its own pleasures, as the explorer Frederick Cook discovered:

> The clouds were at first violet, but they quickly caught the train of colors which was spread over the sky beyond. There were spaces of gold, orange, blue, green, and a hundred harmonious blends, with an occasional strip like a band of polished silver to set the colors in bold relief. Precisely at twelve o' clock a fiery cloud separated, disclosing a bit of the upper rim of the sun.

The pioneering Australian navigator Harold Gatty referred to the smells of rosemary off Spain, peat off the Falklands, and orange groves off the islands of Cape Verde. It is something that all sailors who have spent time away from land will have experienced. There is a well-known connection between smell and memory, which is made more poignant by the fact that our sense of smell peaks in middle age and then deteriorates as we get older. Alert and focused humans will still only manage to sense a very limited olfactory world, "like color-blind men gazing at a painting full of subtle nuances of color." But even within our human limits, it is too easy to let a wealth of detail pass by. This is partly about sense and partly about deduction. If we are on land and smell the sea, the typical response is limited to a general positive reaction, "I can smell the sea!" If we tune our senses and try to make a more detailed deduction we might note that there is a strong whiff of seaweed in the sea smell, which denotes that it is likely to be low tide: The seaweed on the beach has been exposed to the elements. The very fact that we are smelling it indicates an onshore breeze, very possibly a sea breeze. This in turn suggests that there may be a wind direction reversal to a land breeze as the day ends and the night cool draws in. "I can smell the sea" becomes "I suspect that I know what the wind and water are doing!"

The human ability to use smell to understand territory is weak compared to most animals, but not nonexistent. We might come to know urban areas relative to the most striking smell signposts, such as a sewage works. There is a street market on North End Road in west London that sells a lot of fruit and fresh produce. This may be what attracts the seagulls in such numbers. It leads to an unusual sensory map of the area that includes the sight and sound of the gulls, but the street itself smells different at different times of the day and year. Early on a winter day there is no way of telling how close you are to the market by smell, but late on a summer day the scent of overripe fruit that has been trampled on the roads and pavements carries several hundred yards downwind.

This relationship between temperature and smell can be used in a rural context, too. There is a distinct difference between the smell of open country and woodland, and this can be used to find your way out of the woods if you pick it up on the breeze. It is also occasionally possible to find an opening in woodland from temperature and smell. If the sun is bright and the wind light, but not still, then very occasionally it is possible to sense a pocket of slightly warmer air that is richer in smell. This is where the opening in the wood has allowed sunlight in to warm the vegetation and create a stronger smell.

In wilderness areas the most unusual smells will be a clue to humans, other animals, or changes in the environment. The desert smells very clean until humans, animals, or water are introduced, all three often coming together at an oasis and giving off a relatively strong smell and the buzz of thousands of flies. Our taste buds are most sensitive to sweet, sour, salt, and bitterness. Nearly everything else is determined by our sense of smell. Different meats taste the same if we hold our nose, and so it is best to think of the two senses, taste and smell, as working in tandem. It is possible, with care, to tell whether a waterway is freshwater or tidal seawater from its salinity. If you are following a stream hoping to emerge from the wild nearer the coast, then this may be of some help.

Horace Beck, the American collector and author of nautical folklore, tells a wonderful story of an old sailor who could reputedly tell where he was by tasting the sounding lead after it had been hauled off the bottom of the seabed. On a foggy day the crew decided to trick him, and when he was not watching they dipped the lead into some hen manure and passed it to him:

> First he looked at it, then he smelled and finally tasted it. He became very excited and shouted, "Luff up, boys, luff up! Something's terrible wrong! Accordin' to the lead, we're in the middle of Mrs Murphy's hen yard on Smith Island!"

Sounds form an integral part of a landscape and journey. The best evidence of our ability in this area comes when we learn from those who have been deprived of the sense of sight. Blind people use a stick for the sense of touch, but also to gauge echoes.

The effectiveness of echoes is easy to test for ourselves, even without the refined awareness that long-term blindness brings. On my courses I ask a volunteer to walk in silence, with their hands behind their back and their eyes shut, toward a wall until they feel uncomfortably close. Next I ask them to do the same thing while making a constant noise, "*la-la-la-la-la.*" They typically manage to get more than a foot closer to the wall when making the noise. This is of course the principle behind radar and echo sounders, but it has been used in a practical way long before that. The timed echo of a whistle in Puget Sound was used by the navigator in fog to gauge how far the cliffs were. The timbre of the echo gave clues as to the exact bluff or cliff off of which it was bouncing. A variation of this method has been used by explorers in polar regions to gauge the thickness of ice, as was noted by one of Captain Robert Scott's polar companions, Apsley Cherry-Garrard, in the Antarctic: "We sounded all about and everywhere was hollow." Ben Underwood, who lost his sight to retinal cancer at the age of three, learned how to walk and even rollerblade around his home area, inside and out, by using echoes. He was totally blind, but he could point to cars or dustbins in the street from a distance by picking up their echoes from the clicking sound he made with his mouth. He could even play table football and video games by understanding the sounds better than others.

Another beautiful example of using our ears to navigate comes from British army officer F. Spencer Chapman's experiences with the Inuit in Greenland. He watched them navigate their way in kayaks along the coast in fog, using birdsong to identify where their home fjörd was.

Buoys with bells have been used for centuries to help mariners in fog. The criminal mind of the wrecker worked out a valuable, if morbid, source of income. They would row out to the buoys and damp them by stuffing a rag into the bell, then lie in wait. The ship's crew would listen nervously for a bell that had fallen silent before the ship foundered on the shore and the wreckers could pick it clean.

On land the sound of water may mean a river is near, but it might also be able to reveal something about the shape of the land itself. Water flows downhill, of course, but sound does not travel well through the ground itself. The sounds we hear will be determined by our height, as well as the contours of the land around us.

Sounds carry differently over varying surfaces, both in distance and quality. The sounds that we make change on differing surfaces, too. Our footsteps can reveal clues about the moisture of the ground we walk over. A simple "squelch" can yield clues about the orientation of a path.

The Australian Aboriginals have long used their ears to understand journeys in a unique way. Their "songlines" mapped the territory around them in a series of songs and stories, some of which are still in use today. Each part of a song corresponds with an important landmark, such as a ridge or source of water. By recalling the right song the land can be navigated with greater familiarity and, thanks to the sense of hearing, the memory and experience of their journeys lives on beyond their destination.

The sensations of the ground underfoot have always been a delight for sailors returning to shore, but also for those who have been on the ice for too long. Robert Scott felt this acutely: "A lot could be written on the delight of setting foot on rock after fourteen weeks of snow and ice and nearly seven out of sight of aught else."

The contrasts are often much subtler. The difference between one side of a ridge and another may have been generated by millions of years of erosive forces, but that may only translate into the tiniest change underfoot, from a coarse to a fine scree. There are some paths that feel different on each side, despite looking identical. These paths might have one side that is more exposed to the prevailing wind than the opposite side, thinning the soil and making it feel harsher and more "gravelly" under-foot. When there is a harsh ground frost the sense of touch can sometimes help, even in pitch darkness. Paths are usually mar-ginally higher or lower than the surrounding ground, and when warmer daytime breezes come to thaw the ground, paths tend to retain or lose their frost at a different rate from the ground on either side. It is sometimes possible to follow a lower path, in the dark, by keeping the crunchy feel of frozen grass underfoot.

It is not always what we can feel, but what we cannot, that trig-gers our senses. The Antarctic explorer Frederick Cook sensed danger in stillness. When we become accustomed to a sensation, like a biting wind, its absence can make us uneasy, a prompt for us to be alert to the fact that something in our environment has changed.

Not all sensations are external. We are more likely to be able to understand where we have traveled if we walk it ourselves than if we are carried—even if we are deprived of all our external senses. The feeling of muscle contractions can give clues about direction and distance. This "kinesthetic" ability is something that we have all experienced in a general sense: We can tell the difference in feeling in our legs between a one-mile walk and a ten-mile one, but it is not something that we give as much attention to as we might.

When important natural clues like the sun disappear, then the senses must be relied on to their fullest. If the sun vanishes behind clouds, it does not mean that all trace of it has disappeared. It is possible to "remember" where it was by touching two sides of a large boulder. One side will retain warmth for a long time after the sun has gone in, the exact length of time depending on the type of rock.

Although not one of the five senses, time is integral to navigation. Most of us will have proved to ourselves that it is possible to sharpen our natural awareness of time. Everyone who has gone a few weeks or months of their lives without wearing a watch will likely have noticed that their "inner clock" starts to run more accurately.

Experiments going back to 1935 have demonstrated this ability. Humans deprived of all external time clues are able to gauge time accurately with only about a ten-minute error per twenty-four hours. Our ability to gauge time using external references like the sun is therefore a lot better than most of us imagine. More recent research has found that our ability to gauge time alters with age. Our perception of minutes, days, and months changes as we age, but they also feel different to us as we grow older. Our time on this planet seems to shape our understanding of time itself.

Time is part of nature. Units of time are only definitions of natural phenomena that occur in those parcels. A second was defined as 1⁄86,400th of a day (60 x 60 x 24) and then measured using a 39-inch pendulum. Time is meaningless without natural phenomena.

There is evidence of water clocks being used in Babylonian times, and a sundial could be found in the forum at Rome from the third century BC onward. The sundial had its grandest moment with the erection of a seventy-five-foot-high one by Augustus in the first century AD. It now stands in the Piazza di Montecitorio in Rome. Use of the sun to gauge time can still be seen in cultures that do not rely upon modern technology. In the Kalahari Desert, members of the Gwi tribe measure time in days and fractions of days by pointing to where the sun will be at the time they mean on the day in question. The people of the Mursi tribe in Ethiopia count days between planting time and the harvest by tying knots in a cord around their ankles. This type of technique is of great interest to the natural navigator because of the relationship between time and distance. Modern walkers still measure distance using time. The question, "How far is it?" from one walker to the next is often answered by, "An hour." Rather than, "Three miles." Sailors have traditionally talked in terms of the number of "days' sail." Scott used a combination of time and knowledge of his animals to mark distance in the Antarctic: "We are at Number Fourteen Pony Camp, only two pony marches from One Ton Depot."

There is an important aspect to the consideration of time for the natural navigator that is more philosophical than practical. In the Pacific, the traditional oceanic navigators would aim to arrive at any new island in daylight unless they knew it intimately. If there was any risk of coming across land unexpectedly at night they would heave-to and wait for dawn the following morning before continuing. This is not a concept that the contemporary Western mind has to tackle very often. Imagine driving to a friend's house, but when it gets dark more quickly than you expected it to you park by the side of the road, go to sleep, and continue the following morning.

Learning to understand nature takes time. It is not something best approached with firm schedules or a particular deadline. Natural navigators will regularly set out hopeful of returning with some new knowledge in one area and return with something else, which they had not been seeking. Perhaps it is near the summer solstice, and you set out early in the morning to watch the early sun, thinking that it is a good time of year to get a feel for its bearing. But you return, late, having been waylaid by thoughts about a spiders web in the lee of a gatepost.

A lot of the enjoyment of the subject is to be had in lateral thought and mental detours. This is helped enormously by an old-fashioned approach to time. It is much better to go for a walk that happens to take half an hour than to go for a half-hour walk.

It is time for us to take the first steps.

CHAPTER 1

Vale and Dune: The Land

The most common method for finding direction on land relies on the traveler's familiarity with the landscape itself. This is known as landmark navigation. Young men of the Tuareg, a Berber nomadic people who are the principal inhabitants of the Sahara Desert, tend goats from a very early age. They are given clear guidelines as to the range within which they and the goats are allowed to go. This area is then extended steadily in order to mold the herders' instinct. Over time, they learn to find their way over a large area without any formal training in the art of navigation. A very similar method of learning is experienced by all of us as we come to know our own home area. All of us make countless routine journeys each day, and the methods we apply in navigating our way through known territory can equally apply to journeys made through unknown lands.

An important childhood lesson is that getting lost is not much fun. From ancient wilderness to supermarket aisles, few people have reached adulthood without some memories of being disoriented and the accompanying fear. At the heart of this experience is the realization that if one strays from family or ventures away from home, one needs to be able to get back. This is one of the simplest of navigational philosophies: If you can find your way back safely, knowledge about the direction of the outward journey is a lot less critical and can often be dispensed with.

Learning this forms a fundamental part of human development, and is woven into our culture. Children grow up with tales like that of Hansel and Gretel, the two children who become lost in the woods and are captured and fattened up by a cannibalistic witch. The story delivers a strong moral: Getting lost can end in terror. Knowing that there is a need to get back is not enough; it is the ability to find the *way* back that is crucial. Hansel and Gretel were aware that they needed to be able to find their way home, but failed because the trail of breadcrumbs they left behind them was eaten by the birds.

Age brings with it experience and greater abilities, but the challenge remains. The stories that adults enjoy continue to reflect our fear of being lost. On the island of Crete the Minotaur, a half-bull, half-man monster, lived at the heart of a complex labyrinth. Each year Minos, the king of the island, demanded that the Athenians feed the Minotaur seven boys and seven maidens to avenge the death of his son at their hands. One year the Athenian hero Theseus decided to put an end to this and asked to be delivered to the Minotaur as one of the sacrificial boys. He made his way into the labyrinth and successfully slew the Minotaur. If Theseus had acted alone this may have been the end of him as well as the monster, since this was as far as he had planned. Fortunately, he had an accomplice. He was able to escape the labyrinth and survive only because the princess Ariadne had shown him how to find his way back out of the maze by following a thread she gave to him.

The woods of childhood become the Cretan labyrinth, and the breadcrumbs become the thread, but the moral—and the fear—remain.

If myth and legend help illustrate the perils of getting lost and the importance of navigating the return journey, they are less effective at demonstrating any practical and effective methods of retracing the same route.

A more practical method than leaving thread or breadcrumbs is to in some way alter the landscape itself. Trail blazing is the process of marking a path at various points, creating markers that then assist on the return journey and on subsequent visits. This takes many forms, from leaving chalk markings to broken branches. Signposts are themselves just highly evolved trail blazes.

In most areas of open country it is possible to find evidence that those who have gone before us have subtly changed the appearance of the landscape. The Inuit in the Arctic left *inuksuit*, mounds of stone, to indicate good hunting areas and also a guide to the safest way home, while Captain Scott did the same in the Antarctic. Cairns have been used by the American Indians, the nomads of Mongolia, and across the mountain ranges of Europe, America, and Asia. In one of the many incidents that lend authenticity to Cormac McCarthy's postapocalyptic novel, *The Road*, the protagonists come across cairns that have been left by survivors fleeing a dying town.

At other times and places a different solution might be used. The Aboriginals of Australia traditionally lit spinifex grass fires that indicated the way from a considerable distance. When you drive along a straight road in Europe, it is possible that it is an old

Roman road, built with the help of fires to signal the route. Trail blazes, cairns, and fires have been set up to stand out from nature, to become visible against the landscape around them for a good reason. Finding direction by reading the land can be difficult and even dangerous. Today's travelers are fortunate in that modern instruments have allayed some of that immediate danger, but in many ways modern navigational tools do not make the task of reading the land easier; if anything they have made this much more difficult by conditioning the traveler's focus away from the land itself.

A compass contains no information about the landscape its owner is moving through. Satellite navigation maps strip out much detail, sometimes leaving only public roads in their reds, yellows, and greens against a banal beige. This is only the latest in a long cultural development, from Greek philosopher and geographer Anaximander's first map of the world, created in 550 BC, that has proved that it is possible to convey information about the location of a place without the need to convey a sense of the place itself. This has been a powerful development, but its very success has led to a strangely limited perspective of the world and the journey itself.

The largest scale map becomes featureless in the world of sounds, temperature, textures, colors, and smells. This may lead to a belief that these features are irrelevant to a journey. Perhaps we even cease to believe that they exist.

On May 17, 1984, Marvin Creamer sailed into Cape May harbor in New Jersey, having completed a sailing circumnavigation of the world without the assistance of navigational instruments. He would seem an unlikely person to think of in relation to the land, but his understanding of the natural world was shaped early on, when his feet were still dry, and must have helped foster a fascination in the methods he would later use very effectively at sea. Early in his account of the voyage he writes:

> Farm life for a growing boy was fun. Chirping frogs told you when it was time to get rid of long underwear, the throbbing call of the Whip-poor-will beckoned you to shed your shoes and feel the freshly turned earth between your toes. The sequent blooms of arbutus, violets, laurel, lady slippers, honeysuckle, and magnolias provided a calendar guide for closing school and getting plants started for the summer's crops.

Navigating naturally on land is about reintroducing a childlike curiosity to the journey. It is about learning to take note of the things that do not always appear on maps and sensations which are not easily recorded. It is about reconnecting with the land, and in doing so, keeping at bay the feelings of bewilderment and fear that getting lost can bring, on the outward journey and the return one.

Reading the Land

There are two key foundation stones to reading the land. One is learning to interpret the effects of sun, wind, and water. The other is gaining an appreciation of the importance of scale.

Useful clues can be on a distant horizon or just inches away. This means that it is necessary to keep the senses scouring, shifting focus constantly, which requires conscious effort, but yields plenty of rewards. The natural navigator puts more into a land journey than other travelers, but returns with a basketful of observations and sensations that pass others by: the valley that comes to life with the sound of water over rocks being carried by a breeze—all of this has been felt, has been understood.

The effects of sun, wind, and water are ubiquitous. Sometimes it is obvious: the outline of the coast, seen from a hilltop. At other times their effects are harder to glean—the infinite number of subtly different shades of bark color. This is where science and art meet, at once tantalizing and frustrating. However hard it might be to decipher the complex information being delivered by our eyes and other senses, it is crucial to remember that within a seemingly random series of events, there will almost certainly be some order, some beautiful, if hard to fathom, logic to it all. All living things rely on the sun and water, even if indirectly, and if their behavior does not reflect the need to harness these two elements, then their chances of survival are lower. Keeping this in mind and using all the senses can help solve many enigmas. A tree on the edge of a city park growing in a way that appears confusing initially may start to make sense when the sunlight bouncing off the tall mirror-glass building on the other side of the road is felt on one cheek.

HILLS, ROCKS, AND RIVERS

The search for distant and closer clues should start from the best position possible. This usually means finding the highest vantage point and then looking all around, as well as up and down.

A good view will help to form a picture of the shape, the patterns, and grain of the land itself. Studying the land will reveal whether it consists of flat open plains or gentle undulations, or perhaps steeper, more dramatic rises and falls to the Earth's surface. High ground will tell a story of geological formation and erosion. In the south of England there is a range of hills called the South Downs, mounds of chalk that have determinedly weathered erosion over millions of years. They form a range that runs broadly west to east, near parallel to the south coast. Once this alignment is understood, one can make simple deductions. If the sea can be seen, then there must be some south in the view, but if the land slopes away continuously to low country it must be close to north. To the east and west the ridge continues across rolling summits without losing height. I use this example to demonstrate how it is possible to learn the characteristics and features of a range of hills, to read their text. Some, like the Biligiriranga Hills, in India, follow a very straight line, others are more sinuous and therefore present more of a challenge. It takes time to become familiar with a new range of hills, but they all yield their secrets eventually. When they do, it can become possible to walk a long way in a chosen direction with no other aid.

The shape and alignment of hills and valleys can yield directional clues, but the character of the hills themselves can also be influenced by aspect. The southern side of any range of hills in the northern hemisphere will experience a greater variety of temperature than the northern side. In winter, the southern side of a hill may go through repeated frost and thaw cycles, while the northern side, hidden from the warmth of the sun, remains consistently frozen. In mountainous regions like the Alps this difference is drawn by the varying heights of the snow line. This leads to greater erosive forces on the southern side, often giving it a different look and feel.

On a smaller scale, burrowing animals like moles tend to prefer damper, softer, more malleable mud that can be found on the shaded slopes, and this can lend a darker, rougher appearance to one side of a grassy hill. Sometimes the general effect is detectable from a distance, but the detail can only be seen close up. In the summer in particular, shaded areas retain moisture longer: A grassy slope that has a darker appearance from a distance may reveal a few small dark circles closer up, giving the whole slope a darker hue. Inspecting these dark patches close up in turn will reveal much smaller culprits, like a writhing army of ants enjoying the ground that has been kept shady, cool, and moist.

Hills and rivers have a symbiotic relationship; water is channeled by land but then carves into that land over time. It is impossible to understand one without the other. While the Pennines (a range of mountains that traverses northern England and southern Scotland) run north–south, there are rivers in the Pennines, like the Ure and its accompanying valley of Wensleydale, that run west–east off them.

The need to understand the character of the land in a particular area is an ancient one, often reflected in myth and legend. In one part of the Kalahari Desert, a valley and the minerals found there are explained by a myth about a creature called Gamama. Gamama was bitten by a snake, and as it dragged its injured leg, it gouged out the valley. Then the snakebite brought on a fever, and Gamama vomited. The vomit dried as the visible minerals.

Water, in its solid form of ice, has shaped large areas of land through the movement of glaciers and ice sheets. Within the broader effects of this ice flow, there are occasionally more distinct patterns that can be read. The shape of the land can betray the direction of the long-departed ice and can in turn be used to find direction. In County Armagh, Northern Ireland, there are a series of small hills known as "drumlins," from the Gaelic word for hills, that have been shaped by the retreating ice and appear elongated along the axis that the ice has flowed, in this case south–north. Where the ice remains it cloaks the land and makes the task harder, but not impossible. In the Antarctic, Sir Ernest Shackleton learned to read the shape of the land through the ice sheets and crevasses themselves.

Where there is little water, the geology becomes of greater importance. The desert-dwelling Bedouin of the Arabian Peninsula come to know intimately the shape of rock outcroppings and to recognize patterns where others would see none. In the 1960s,

←————————————————— Direction of ice flow

Retreating ice sculpts the land and leaves clues to direction.

the British explorer and writer John Hillaby led a caravan of camels over 600 miles across the North Kenyan desert to Lake Rudolph. At one stage he used a lava wall as his guide, but then left it when it turned east and he wanted to go south.

Once a relationship with the local land and water has been developed, it is time to look at the ground itself. When looking at the land in detail, scale of distance and time are important, since not only the geological forces of millions of years, but also differences that appear over several hours as the result of the elements can be witnessed. In either case the search is for trends and biases. The most obvious and frequently changing of these biases can be seen in the relationship between the sun and moisture levels.

PUDDLES

Puddles have much to teach us about the way the land can be read and how deductions about the arc of the sun can be used to find direction. They are easily accessible repositories of information.

Nearly all country tracks and paths have an incline of some sort on each side. Very often there will be some plant growth on either side, too, sometimes only short grass, at other times burgeoning undergrowth, bushes, or even trees. As the sun moves through the sky each day it casts its shadows on the path and the position of these shadows can cause some parts of the track to dry more slowly than others. A path that heads north–south will receive roughly equal amounts of drying sunlight on each side, since the sun rises on one side of it and sets on the other. The drying is evened out over the course of the average day. However, in the northern hemisphere the sun spends most of its time in

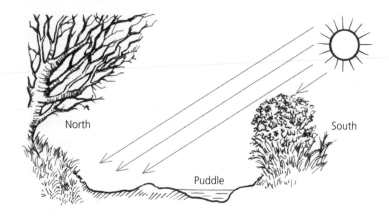

Puddles take longer to dry on the southern side of west–east paths in the northern hemisphere

the southern part of the sky, which means that on an east–west path, the incline and growth on the southern side of the track will cast a shadow on the southern part of the track itself. Moisture is retained, puddles last longer.

Over time there is often a compounding effect. Walkers or vehicles pass through country lanes and the softer southern side of the track is therefore more easily worn. The next time the rain falls, the southern side gathers more water than the northern side, and the cycle begins again. In summer, the puddles may have evaporated away, but their effect can still be read in the shape of the dry mud and often in a shade difference between two sides of a path. The result is that east–west paths can look very different from north–south paths, and the junctions between the two will often reveal a stark change.

A detail that is nearly always overlooked is the color of puddles. Occasionally it is possible to spot a marked difference between each end of one particular puddle, perhaps a translucent muddy water at one end and an opaque pale green at the other. This effect can be caused by plant matter or algae near the surface of the puddle being blown to one end by a prevailing wind. In the UK, the prevailing wind is from the southwest, and will push at the surface of the water of a puddle, so that the northeastern end will sometimes reveal a shade of green when the southwest does not.

In the early stages of learning to navigate naturally, time spent investigating puddles is rarely wasted. The key is always to think about the surroundings, to understand the sun's effect, getting to know its different arc in summer and winter, thinking about the shape of the surrounding ground, the wind, and rain, and then trying to understand what can be deduced. Jumping to the conclusion that puddles will always be found on the southern side of the track without going through this process will sometimes be wrong. And, equally importantly, the enjoyment of the investigation will have been missed.

The humble puddle tells a story of sun, wind, and water that helps point the way. It is a story that is seldom read these days.

The Plants

In 1771 the English polymath Joseph Priestley let a candle burn in a sealed container until its flame dampened down and finally extinguished. He then placed a small mint plant into the same container. After a few days he noticed that there was again "gas" within the container, of a sufficient quantity to support the candle flame again. He had discovered that plants produce oxygen, as a by-product of photosynthesis, the process whereby plants convert sunlight and water into energy in the form of glucose. This process is made possible through the presence of chlorophyll, found in the chloroplasts, the photoreceptors of green plants. Photosynthesis explains why the presence or absence of sunlight has an enormous impact on the growth of plants, and this knowledge can in turn be used for navigation. More available energy leads to denser growth and is therefore usually found in plants which receive more sunlight. This can be observed in different ways, over vast areas of land or in the branches of a single tree.

Plants, and especially trees, give an area its own unique look and feel. The trees that are prospering will tell us much about the soil, climate, and exposure to the elements. Different species tolerate different levels of sun and wind. Seen from above, almost the whole length of Sweden is dominated by spruces and pines. Spruces rule the south, and pines hold court in the north. This has led to a booming paper industry and in some regions the sweet and sour stink of a paper factory announces that a town is near.

On a smaller, more immediate scale, the sunnier side of hill slopes will often have denser plant growth than the shaded side. The sunnier slopes will also host the plants that are more energy hungry. One simple trick that can be useful in the northern hemisphere is to remember "sweet is south." The availability of sunlight has a bearing on the amount of energy a plant produces, in the form of glucose or sugar. This means that sweet fruits, like grapes and peaches, tend to favor the slopes that get the most sun, the south-facing ones in the northern hemisphere.

A field of blooming crops that stretches over uneven ground, perhaps over the crest of a hill, will betray direction. The crops in the field will not all prosper or come into bloom simultaneously, and their timing will be influenced not only by the quality of the soil but also by the levels of sunlight and wind. In this way, information can be deduced from a reading of the land. A field of rapeseed may come into brilliant yellow bloom first in the corner that has a southern aspect and some shelter from the wind. This will also be the corner that first reverts to green. These greens and yellows can spread across an undulating field to form a color compass.

Zooming in further still, the effect of photosynthesis can be seen within individual plants themselves. Plants do not have a central nervous system, which means that their individual parts have to act and react autonomously, so that each leaf, stem, and branch can behave independently of the plant as a whole.

There are plants that react surprising quickly to the light. Heliotropic plants—those which track the sun's motion from east to west across the sky—like the alpine buttercup and others found in high latitudes, rely on getting as much of the low light as they can during daylight hours.

It is not only heliotropic plants which show an urgent and understandable interest in the sun's direction. Many plants display what is known as leaf heliotropism. The nasturtium leaf, for example, has an organ at its base which enables it to tilt itself at right angles to the sun and track it during the day. Ivy finds itself with conflicting objectives: One part, the stem, tends to grow toward the shade where support from trees is more likely, while its leaves need the sunlight.

As a general rule, however, the longer term the effect of the sun, the more dependable it will be for navigation. A flower that points to the sun is not adding much to the cause if the sun is clearly visible. A plant that can reveal where the sun has been over time, even at night or on an overcast day, is far more valuable for navigation. The flowers of many plants show a preference for certain aspects, most typically between south and east. The flowers of the giant cactus of Tucson, Arizona, for example, show a predilection for the eastern side of the plant, where the sun reaches first and warms the cold air from the previous night. When the nineteenth-century American poet Henry Wadsworth Longfellow wrote, "Look at this delicate flower that lifts its head from the meadow, See how its leaves all point to the North as true as the magnet," he was likely referring to the prairie weeds and wild lettuces of the United States that do indeed align themselves north–south. The "North Pole" plant of South Africa, *Pachypodium namaquanum,* is a large succulent with a crowned head that reliably points north.

A more common bias, one that is not so species specific, is often present in the body of a plant. If one side shows a pronounced denser growth, or heaviness, then it is likely that it is receiving more light.

Discerning a pattern of growth on smaller plants may be difficult, but on larger, more established plants, and on trees in particular, the effect can be quite dramatic.

THE TREES

What a great thought of God was that when He thought a tree!

—John Ruskin

Within most landscapes, the ideal tree to study is an isolated one, preferably in an area that is exposed to the elements, but not completely ravaged by them. (Take care not to approach an isolated thorn tree at night though, since according to a Norse myth, they are bewitched, and a "fiery wheel will come forth" and destroy you.)

The problem with looking at trees in woodland, or even just two or three together, is that these trees will be reacting to each other as well as the elements and so the task of unraveling the evidence of elemental influences becomes much more complex. If forced to choose a tree in a wooded area, always go for the "King of the Jungle" the tree that appears tallest, oldest, most established and dominant. This is the one that is most likely to reflect effects of the elements in an unadulterated way. The trees around it have probably had to make bigger compromises—the price of not getting there first.

Environmental adaptations of the type which can be "read" are usually more pronounced on deciduous trees than on evergreens. Evergreens have evolved to cope with low levels of diffuse light over long periods, whereas deciduous trees explode into action for a few months and their leaves tend to be much broader. These two factors can accentuate their reactions. In many areas, of course, evergreens are dominant and therefore must be used, but they are usually harder to read than an oak, ash or beech which stands proudly alone.

Perspective is vital. The most common mistake that newcomers to the art of natural navigation make is to look up at a tree from one angle, trying to read it before they have taken the time to walk around it. If the only available tree is in the distance, on a ridge on the horizon perhaps, then there may be no choice, but whenever possible a full circuit is advisable. A tree becomes four, eight, sixteen different trees from different perspectives and it is these differences that can reveal information about its orientation.

After studying the tree from as many angles as possible, try to ascertain whether it appears "heavier" on one side. Sometimes this effect is pronounced, but often it is necessary to look for subtle differences. Imagine taking a "mental chain saw," sawing a tree in half down the middle of its trunk and then weighing each side in a giant set of scales. In Canada and the northern United States, the side of the scales that hits the ground will likely have a southerly aspect; the more pronounced the difference, the greater the confidence that can be placed in the scales.

The next thing to look for is shape within the tree. Reading a tree, or indeed any plant, is helped by an understanding of phototropism. Phototropism is the directional growth of a plant that is influenced by light. Plants contain chemical messengers or hormones called auxins, which encourage cell elongation within the plant. The ingenious thing about them is that they do not act equally in all places in the plant. Auxins are effectively "pushed" to the opposite side of the stem of a plant by sunlight. These auxins then act on the cells on the side opposite the most light causing them to grow longer, with the result that the stem will bend toward the light.

This effect is seen in individual stems of a particular plant but also in branches on two sides of the same tree. The branches on the lighter side, south in the northern hemisphere, will grow out toward the light, while the branches on the darker side will tend to grow more vertically. This results in the "Check Effect." When viewed from the west, northern hemisphere trees sometimes look as though they have a check mark running across their branches. From the east the effect is a backward check. While the denser growth can usually be spotted in the summer months, the check mark is easier to gauge when a deciduous tree's branches can be seen.

A third effect of the sun on trees can be seen after they have been cut down. Dendrochronology is the science of using tree rings to understand the age of a tree and the climate it experienced during its life. A navigational pointer can be found in a different aspect of the trunk of a felled tree—an architectural

In the northern hemisphere, isolated deciduous trees often show a "heaviness" on their southern side and the "Check Effect" in their branches.

one. If a tree grows more densely on one side than another, then it follows that the trunk which supports this growth will reflect this imbalance. Leonardo da Vinci took time out from inventing flying machines and painting masterpieces to note that the heart of a tree can often be found closer to the southern side than the northern.

It is not only the sun that leaves its mark on a tree. Trees cannot escape the wind, and their shape will reflect this. When looking for the effect of wind on trees it is the trends that are of interest, not the instant effects. (Current wind direction can be judged more easily by the feel and sound of it on cheeks and ears.) A tree can be blown temporarily in any direction during a gale, but its shape will reflect the prevailing wind in an area, the aggregate effect of many days and years. Exposure is critical; a tree in the lee of a hill will often disappoint, but a tall tree on a ridge can sometimes be read from a long way off. For this method it is necessary to know the prevailing wind direction in the local area. In New York, for example, this is from the south-west, so trees will often show a combed effect from the southwest to the northeast. If the prevailing direction is not known, then it is possible to deduce this by using the sun or stars or any other clues to establish direction initially and then comparing the effect on the trees with this. Once established it will be consistent for a wide area.

It is clear that the tree in the illustration opposite has been shaped by a wind that has blown consistently from the left, which in New York means that southwest is likely to be to the left. With practice it becomes straightforward to deduce that the tree is being viewed at right angles to southwest, the observer

The prevailing wind shapes exposed trees as it combs their upper branches and extremities.

is looking from southeast of the tree toward northwest. Most people struggle with this orientation initially, but it becomes easier over time.

Where the winds are particularly strong or the species of tree especially vulnerable, wind can have a thwarting effect. In extreme cases the tree can look as though it has been stripped bare on one side.

As with the effects of the sun, clues provided by exposure to the wind can be found in fallen trees. This is particularly valuable in wooded areas where other clues may be hard to find. Trees fall for many reasons, including disease and weak ground, but the final push often comes from the wind. Several fallen trees in the same area of woodland that appear, from the level of decay, to have come down at a similar time, are very likely to have been toppled by the same gale or storm. Once the direction of this storm's winds are known then these trees will tend on average to fall roughly in line over a wide area. The trees that fell in England in the great storm of 1987 were brought down by winds from between south and southwest. Their decaying trunks can still guide walkers through the woods to this day. This technique would also have worked well in Central Park for a year after the storm in August 2009, when 500 trees were blown over from west to east. Sadly, for natural navigators at least, most of these have now been removed.

The sun and wind do not act independently, but in tandem. Isolated trees will often show a combination of effects, which can make the task of interpretation more challenging or help to reinforce a theory. Before trying to discern the differences between the two, it is worth remembering that the wind will shape things in proportion to how exposed they are. The extremities of trees, the outer edges and the tops, will tend to show more "combing" than the body of the tree. In turn the thick main branches in the body of the tree are more influenced over time by the sun. A dominant wind effect can make any sun effect hard to spot, but the sun's effect will never negate the impressions of a prevailing wind.

The best way to approach this detective work is to let the tree speak, using instinct to gauge which is the more dominant force on a particular tree, the sun or the wind. Then form a hypothesis of direction, by deducing from that effect which way the tree is oriented. Next, try to estimate what is the likely effect from the lesser of the two influences of wind or sun. If a tree appears "heavier" on one side, then that side is probably south. It may be that some combing is discernible in the upper branches that is consistent with the prevailing wind direction in your area, too. If so, then you can assume that your original deduction was right.

At other times it will contradict your theory, and then it is time to start again with a new hypothesis, or abandon that tree for another one, or look elsewhere for one of nature's clues.

If deciphering these clues becomes at times frustrating, it is worth holding on to the idea that nature cannot afford much wasted effort. There is nearly always a reason for what we observe, even if at times that reason eludes us. In the nineteenth century a Scottish writer, James Fergusson, came across an old date tree in Tessore, India, that was behaving in a strange and puzzling way. Crowds were gathering around each day, hanging garlands from its branches and worshipping it. It was believed that one of the gods had appeared in it. This was evident because each morning when the sun rose the tree would raise its head to welcome him. Each evening it would bow its head as the sun set. Dr. Fergusson observed this for himself and then set about searching for an explanation. He concluded that the sun was causing the date tree's twisted trunk to dry and untwist during the day, raising its crown, and then to retract and coil again slightly at night. This gave Fergusson an acceptable scientific explanation, but it did not contradict the Hindu assertion that it was the work of Surya, the Sun God.

MOSSES AND LICHENS

There are over 10,000 moss and 15,000 lichen species in the world, so getting to know them all by name is probably out. However, it can be very helpful to know something about their general preferences, habits, and weaknesses. The best place to start is by challenging one of the most popular natural navigation mantras: "Moss grows on the north side of trees and buildings." It does, sometimes, but it will also grow on every other side. Moss does not care about north, south or any other direction, but it cares greatly about moisture.

There is a direct relationship between moisture levels and the sun's arc. If a tree or building receives an equal amount of moisture in the form of rain on all sides, on average the side facing the sun will dry out quickest. Hence moss is often happier on the moister, northern side in the northern hemisphere. If the moisture element is remembered, then it is hard to go wrong, and it becomes straightforward to work out the reason for moss growing in certain locations. The sun is one of the factors affecting moisture, but not the only one and regularly not the dominant one. If moss is to be used to find direction, then the cause for its growth needs to be worked out, i.e., the reason for the presence of moisture.

Gradient is very important: The faster water runs off a surface, the less likely moss is to find the moisture it craves. This can be seen by comparing moss growth on two roofs of different slopes that both face the same way. It is even more striking on trees where a bend or hollow in the trunk can slow the movement of water and make a happy home for moss, even on a south-facing side of a tree.

Texture is another major factor; a rough broken bark surface acts as a brake on water flowing down the tree and will likely prove a good habitat.

Once shallow gradients and coarse textures have been ruled out, the next cause to be wary of is "ground effect." The ground retains moisture, which means that mosses often thrive close to it, regardless of aspect, and it is best to ignore mosses growing within two feet of ground level.

All of these factors can sometimes be seen on a single tree. A silver birch that has some very smooth and some rough bark and also some twists and bends in the trunk is a good example. There may well be moss close to the ground all around the base of the trunk, giving no clues as to direction. There may be moss on the south side if there is a patch of shallow gradient coarse bark there. However, if there is moss growing on a steep, smooth part of the trunk more than sixty centimeters from the ground this is probably because that side of the tree is sheltered from the drying effects of the sun, and moisture is therefore being retained. And in the northern hemisphere it is most likely that this is occurring on the northern side.

Algae are other moisture-loving organisms often confused for mosses. They can be seen as a thin film, sometimes slimy in appearance, on bark, stone and other surfaces. Like moss, algae usually give clues about the moistness of a surface rather than clearly indicating direction. But this information can then be used to make deductions. Often algae are visible as the greenish tinge to a woodland a few hundred meters away. The north side of woodland often wears this green appearance more noticeably in winter than summer.

If mosses are the oft misunderstood, high profile plants of natural navigation, then lichens are their shy, more complex neighbors. They grow very slowly and can live for a very long time, several thousand years in some places, making them possibly the oldest living things on the planet. The route to navigational assistance from lichens is not through understanding their biology, but by learning to recognize colors and patterns within a local area.

The two main things to note are the surface that the lichen is growing upon and the effects of its environment: sun, wind, and water. The aim is to notice consistencies, perhaps orange and brown lichens that like south-facing masonry or a light green one with dark speckles that favors the southwest of trees, likely enjoying the combination of some sunlight and rain-bearing winds. However the diversity and sensitivity of lichens means that a knowledge of local species and their features will usually be more helpful than an attempt to apply general rules. The only trap to be wary of when studying lichens in a chosen area is extrapolating from one surface type to another: A lichen that prospers on a particular type of stone will reveal nothing about what to expect on bark or even on another type of stone.

Lichens are very sensitive to air quality and are sometimes used by environmental scientists to help gauge pollution levels. They add color and character to stones in rural churchyards, but are a lot fussier nearer to town centers. Chichester has a strange old edifice at its center called the "Chichester Cross," built so that the poor might sell their wares beneath it. It has a clock on its roof, supported by eight buttresses, each of which is exposed to subtly different sun, wind and rain patterns. Each buttress reflects its particular aspect in different colors and patterns of lichen, spots of gold and brown on the southern ones, working through grays and pale greens round to the north. Nobody in Chichester is likely to use these clues to find their way however, as the Cross sits at the junction of North, South, East and West Streets.

The Towns

Emerging from a subway station in a big city and trying to orient oneself from the few clues available can be confusing, but also rewarding. The five senses do not shut down when in a town. It is true that towns present some unique obstacles and some sights and smells that might not warrant further attention, but it can be a gratifying experience to walk around a town or city without your head down and your hands rustling lifeless pieces of paper.

Before we consider some of the navigational methods that can be used in towns, it is worth pausing to consider the ways in which we set about exploring them. Towns are synonymous with hurried, efficient activity, but in among this there are many points of interest for the navigator that can be uncovered with an investment of time and a small dose of eccentricity. In 1926, Stephen Graham described his zigzag approach to exploring Manhattan Island in New York, taking alternate right and left turns, rather than moving on the north–south trajectory of the avenues in this most carefully planned of cities. He reveled in the "surprises and delights and curiosities that the city unfolded to me in its purlieus and alleys and highways and quays."

Individual buildings and houses may manage to seal out nature, but towns themselves are not immune. However great the leaps of architects and builders, the most ambitious edifices are still footnotes to any hills and rivers in a town. Sometimes the best approach is to have a good look at a map of a city before embarking on a journey of exploration, getting a feel for these influences and then putting the map away and trying to read them in the land itself.

Occasionally there is a strong navigational heritage, but one that stems from the sky and not the ground. A perfect north–south line can be drawn in Beijing to line up Tiananmen Square, the Bell and Drum Towers, the Monument to the People's Heroes, and Chairman Mao's memorial. This alignment can be used by the earthbound navigator, even if its inspiration was celestial.

There are marked differences between cities that have grown organically, like London and Paris, and those that have been carefully planned and laid out on a grid, like Canberra or Brasilia. The latter are usually more regular and easier to navigate, but in some ways less intriguing.

It is worth monitoring the behavior of that omnipresent city animal, the human being, in order to gain clues as to location. There are directional flows between transport hubs and work-places or tourist attractions, creating a relationship between the land, the buildings, and the people. Stations can be found by going against the flow of people in the morning and with them in the late afternoon. All these movements are influenced by nature and each other in ways that few give any thought to. The direction that people move will be shaped by time, and that in turn is of course governed by the sun. In the summer people move from office blocks to open spaces at lunch time.

The interplay between people on the move is harder to fathom. People follow other people, routes become established, but there is a certain thrill to be had when the senses indicate that it is time to step away from the crowded main street and take a turn down an empty side street. A fun way to remind ourselves of our influence on each other is to stop on a busy street and just stare upward at the sky. It isn't long before others stop walking for a moment and glance up.

The natural forces are still at work in a town. The sun might cause colors to fade and paint to peel more quickly on one side of a particular street. The rain will tend to hit a building from the direction of the prevailing wind and stain it, corrode it, or encourage moss and algae growth. Weathering is a more intricate phenomenon than might first appear, since different stones react in different ways to the elements, which is good news for the navigator. Rather joyously a research paper has even been published with the title: "Effects of Aspect on Weathering: Anomalous Behavior of Sandstone Gravestones in Southeast England."

The technique to use in reading weathering is similar to that of reading lichens. By becoming familiar with local materials and how they weather, one can gain a useful degree of knowledge about a particular city's weather and aspect. Corrosion or blackening will tend to be found more prominently on either the windward or leeward side of buildings. It is always worth looking up above the ground level of buildings as this is where the elements are able to work most freely.

It is sometimes possible to smell a river, lake, or even a park before it comes into sight, and this is much more meaningful if one has some awareness of wind direction. The wind itself can be used as a navigational tool, even when the traveler is sheltered by tall buildings and it cannot be felt, by watching the clouds pass overhead. Prevailing wind direction often influences the broad layout of a town, particularly if there is a history of industry. The less desirable area of town is often downwind, the eastern end in the UK—hence London's East End.

A dependable modern indicator of direction is the TV satellite dish. These point toward geostationary satellites, which remain over the same point on the earth's surface—usually the equator. The direction they're oriented is generally consistent across large areas, and will tend to be the same for a whole city.

Once you have "tuned" into the direction for your city, these dishes can be a great help.

Most tennis courts are laid out on a north–south alignment in an effort to minimize the effect of the sun's glare. Likely time of play and latitude are also taken into account in some instances. It quickly becomes a dark art. One court constructor considered latitude, the assumption that most players are right-handed, and the sun's direction on each equinox between 3 PM and 4 PM and concluded that 22 degrees off north, toward a northwest–southeast alignment, would be the best position for their court.

Religious buildings have always had a strong relationship with direction as they tend to have as their focus something far away, either in another part of the world or in the heavens—the pyramids, for example, followed celestial cues. Christian churches are usually aligned west to east, with the altar at the eastern end. Mosques have a niche in one wall to show *qiblah*, the direction of the shrine in Mecca, but if that is not obvious, then human observation will work: Muslims always pray in the direction of Mecca.

It is worth noting the alignment of tombs, graves, or memorials, as there is an ancient tradition of giving thought to the way the dead face. Many Christian graves are aligned east–west, so that the dead are ready when "the trumpet shall sound and the dead shall be raised."

It is possible that the need to find our way within modern buildings is bringing nature indoors. Architects give ever more thought to natural light, and this can be seen in the orientation of buildings, but the contents are changing, too. Plants are now being used both to soften the internal environment of large buildings and as a way of signposting different places and functions within. Signs are limited to a small number of languages and often blend into the background, whereas plants stand out in an indoor environment and can communicate to everyone. If a shopping center chooses to hang variegated *Scindapsus* plants over each of the escalators, then shoppers of all nationalities will gradually come to understand what the leaves signify, even if the message has been conveyed subliminally.

As with the natural landscape, there is a reason behind the orientation of most things in a town. It is the natural navigator's task to ask questions about how things are aligned and why.

The Sand

The hot and cold deserts of the world are renowned for their emptiness and their lack of animal and plant life, but the clues that can be used to find direction are not nearly as scarce as the animals or people in these regions.

Most indigenous desert people learn to explore their physical environment from a very young age. They learn to read differences in the landscape and to recognize features that would blend into the background for most. This ability is often learned organically and from so early on that it is not considered a special skill. The Saharan Tuareg find it hard to explain how they find their way, but for them it is easy to cross what may appear to the unaccustomed eye to be a featureless landscape. Asking them how they navigate is like asking how they put one foot in front of the other.

When there is no sand in the desert air, visibility is excellent. This means that the height of the observer's eye can make a huge difference, and every opportunity to gain a little height to gauge one's surroundings should be taken. Even climbing on to a camel can open up a lot more terrain in front of you, as well as making it possible to spot gazelle and other desert animals before you get too close and scare them off.

One key method employed by the Tuareg is the use of smell. The Tuareg rarely stop anywhere without lighting a fire and making a potent pot of sweet green tea. The clean dry air carries the smell of the fires over a long distance and can be picked up very easily if approaching from downwind. Smell carries so well that one way of finding a camp is to walk at right angles to the wind direction until you pick up the smell of smoke and then turn upwind. R. A. Bagnold, founder of the Long Range Desert Group during World War II and a desert pioneer, claimed to have found an oasis from eight miles away by following the smell of a single camel.

Time spent in a desert environment allows a rare and pure proximity to the elements. Although generally an unforgiving and potentially dangerous terrain, it is a friendly one to the natural navigator armed with basic knowledge. And few other places on Earth offer such a clear, uncluttered view of the two preeminent navigational guides: the sun and the stars.

There are challenges associated with using the sun near the middle of the day in the desert, since you will probably be near to the equator, and the sun will therefore be very high in the sky near the middle of the day.

On long walks through plains it becomes instinctive to use your own shadow during the course of the day; over your left shoulder at sunrise to over the right shoulder at sunset on a long northerly trek. This friendly shadow is reassuring if the ground suddenly changes consistency or color, which happens surprisingly frequently in the desert and can be very disorienting.

The effects of the sun can be used to differentiate between otherwise identical-seeming dunes in the distance. The sun heating shallower dune slopes will give them a bluish hue, making them stand out from the sand all around. One such blue patch helped me hold a course for over two hours on one occasion. After seven hours of walking in the Takyomet region of the Fezzan Sahara, near the Libyan border with Algeria, I had become separated from the camels that were carrying my extra water. There were mirages teasing my thirst and the dunes started to resemble each other. I was with experienced Tuareg and in no danger, but it was disorienting and dispiriting terrain. Then I noticed a light patch, different from most of the mirages, more steady. It looked like a light blue ski slope in the distant dunes. It was easy to organize the land around this blue sand and this renewed my relationship with direction and gave me energy.

When the sun goes down, the desert can become shockingly alien. It is quite easy to return to a spot that you know well by day and not recognize it at all at night. Very subtle changes in low light levels, especially from the moon, completely redraw the landscape in our minds, almost minute by minute. But at night, the stars are a great comfort and easily found. In the low latitude northern deserts, such as North Africa, it is often possible to see both Polaris and the Southern Cross simultaneously, providing a strong feeling of navigational security.

The lack of precipitation in the desert means that surface particles are not subject to erosion from water and can be left undisturbed for long periods. It is easy to find vehicle tracks in the Sahara Desert that date back to World War II. If you are following someone on foot or in a vehicle, getting to know their prints well is a very good idea, as this will allow you to follow them easily, even when they drop out of sight.

In the absence of water, wind is the decisive influence over the contours of the land in the desert. Trees and grasses in gullies (also known as wadis in the Middle East) and oases still reveal the prevailing effects, with one exception. It is important to differentiate between a prevailing wind and a sand-laden wind. This is especially true when encountering the "lee effect"—the tendency for small particles to fall from an airflow and accumulate on the downwind side of an obstruction. A wind can blow more consistently from one direction over the course of years, but during this time sandstorms might whip up and blow for a couple of days from a different direction. This can lead to conflicting clues: trees that bend one way, while sand deposited in the lee of grasses, i.e. the downwind side, indicates a different direction. The lee effect is generally easier to find, not least because evidence of sandstorms can be found all over the desert, whereas trees are relatively rare.

The method with the lee sand is very similar to that when using fallen trees in woodland: Once you have established the direction that the last sand-depositing winds blew from, then you have a method that will work for many miles, sometimes leaving clues behind each pebble and other tiny obstructions. Each time a sandstorm blows through, it is time to reset this compass.

In the absence of trees, however, there are other clues to prevailing wind direction. Sand and other particles carried by the wind erode the rocks that stand in their way, which can be seen in a gentle weathering effect or even lead to streamlined rock formations called yardangs. Facing the wind is a steep tapered face that gradually gets lower toward the lee end. The direction of this weathering will remain constant over large areas.

Another clue worth looking for is color. Sand comes in a variety of colors, including blacks, purples, and greens, but in the desert it is likely to consist of subtle variations of yellows, oranges, and pinks. The different colors reflect the different chemicals present in the composition of the sand, the varying levels of iron oxide in particular. This can provide a clue that one type is heavier than another type and will behave slightly differently when blown around obstacles. In a few places this leaves a basic color compass, pinker sand on one side and yellower sand on another side of a road, for example.

Clues to understanding the desert's unique riddles lie in its sand dunes. The dunes stand as a record of the relationship between sand, wind, and topography over very long periods of time.

If a desert has one prevailing wind direction, then the sand will likely form nice straightforward barchan dunes. These are crescent-shaped dunes with horns that point in the direction the wind is blowing. If there is no shortage of sand, then a constant wind direction will eventually form transverse dunes. These are enormous ripples in the sand with ridges that are perpendicular to the wind direction, like waves in the sea. Converging winds can create linear or "seif" dunes with ridges that run parallel to the mean wind direction. Seif dunes can reach 300 meters in height and stretch for 200 kilometers in places like the Rub'al-Khali Desert in the Arabian Peninsula.

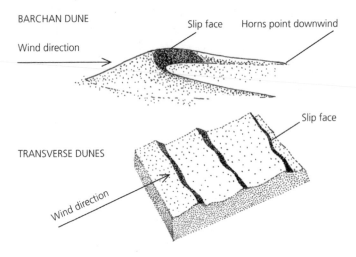

Some sand dunes yield clues to the prevailing wind direction.

A complex dune is created by winds that come from many different directions, and it lives up to its name. They can consist of a mix of different dune types on top of each other, sometimes with a star-shaped dune on top. For all their beauty, complex dunes are hard to fathom. It is sometimes impossible to separate the movement of sand and the wind since the dunes may have become large enough to channel the wind themselves. This can be seen in the ripples in the surface of the dune sand that mold themselves around the dune and illustrate curves in the airflow. Large complex dunes and ranges are best treated in the same way as ranges of hills: They can serve as very useful landmarks even if their full history is hard to read.

The relationship between wind and sand remains important even if it is not used to find direction. The ridgeline of most dunes separates the windward from the leeward side, the former being a shallower slope of harder packed sand, the latter a steeper wall of sand that does not support weight. Walking on the windward side is essential to avoid exhausting and futile stumbling about on the "slip face."

The intensity of the desert environment often leads people to believe that they present perplexing navigational challenges, but for natural navigation they are in many ways easier to grapple with than a walk in the woods.

Ice and Snow

The Arctic and Antarctic do not lack light, during their summer at least, but they never see a high sun. Even on Midsummer's Day in either hemisphere, the sun moves along a shallow gradient, low in the sky. At the poles, the sun does not rise or set, but moves in a circle that notches higher or lower each day as the Earth orbits the sun.

I have been fortunate enough to see the midnight sun on the summer solstice after my flight into the Arctic Circle in 2005. At such high latitudes, the change in light levels is very gradual, while at the equator, the sun can take a couple of minutes to set from the moment it touches the horizon. In high latitudes, the sun's path is near the horizontal and so the change in the sun's height is so slight over time that even when it does dip below the horizon, it is more of a sunslide than a sunset.

The stars have a limited navigational role in high latitudes for two reasons. First, travel tends to be undertaken during very long summer days and, second, the stars themselves are harder to use in high latitudes. The North Star will often be too high in the sky to be a useful guide, and the stars close to the horizon change bearing too quickly to be used to hold a course for long. The reasons why the stars behave in this way are explained in the Firmament chapter.

In the many accounts of polar exploration there is strong evidence to suggest that our senses become more finely tuned the greater the degree of deprivation that they are forced to endure. Considering the sense of sight, what other than brilliant white is there to be found in such wastelands? And yet a quick skim through a number of such memoirs reveals the following vivid descriptions: buttercup-yellow mountains, cobalt and emerald snow crystals, a crimson moon, mint-green icebergs, amber eyes, and velvety-orange Emperor penguins. The eyes play tricks, too: A young Roald Amundsen was once sent out on to the Antarctic ice to greet a unexpected stranger. In the distance the crew of the *Belgica* thought they could see a man carrying a lantern. Amundsen returned to the mystified crew, telling them that what they'd seen was a mass of snow covered with phosphorescent sea algae, emitting light as ice rubbed up against ice.

Wind and Snow

Snow and ice share a relationship with the wind analogous to that between sand and wind. There are comparable wave, ridge, and ripple formations created as the wind sculpts the snow and forms regular patterns in the ice. Snow can form barchan dunes in the same way that sand does.

The wind organizes fresh snow into drifts and lines with one end that points into the prevailing wind. This alignment can be read easily by the Inuit and other indigenous people in northern regions. Fresh snow is also deposited on the leeward side of any obstacles. This latter method can be used even in temperate climates. In February 2009, we endured and enjoyed heavy snow across the UK. I set out on a night walk into the South Downs to catch the snowfall while it was still fresh. I found my way through a beech wood, stomping happily through thick fresh snow, guided by the thin lines of lee snow clinging in strips to the north-northeast of the trees.

In higher latitudes, jagged ridges, called *sastrugi* (from the Russian word for waves), are formed as the prevailing wind sculpts the snow and ice. These sharp edges align with the wind and will remain constant in direction for as long as the wind does.

Each wind has its own characteristics and leaves different marks in the snow. The Inuit have learned to read the various clues on the ground, but have also come to know the different ice formations from the winds that shape them quite personally. One mild and steady wind is called Niqiq and is attributed with a male character, while Uangnaq blows hard and then dies down before whipping up again, and is said to be female. (I suspect that this convention was initiated by the male Inuit.)

The key with reading all wind-formed clues is to remember that cumulative effects, even if they are the result of only a few hours, will tend to be more reliable than using the wind itself. The wind can shift over the course of a few minutes, but sastrugi will not be bent and even snow in a lee will take time to shift.

Another important clue is provided by gazing up at the sky in high latitudes. The undersides of low clouds will appear lighter or darker than normal, depending whether there is open water or ice in the distance. This was explained rather poetically by the polar explorer Frederick Cook:

> A water-sky, a land blink, or some other sign, indicative of land or open water, is constantly before us and these are to the polar explorer, like the Star of Bethlehem to the children of Israel. They perpetually urge us on.

The Arctic plays with the light in one more way that can be helpful. Layers of differing air temperature cause mirages or "looming," when the light refracts and land below the horizon "pops up" above it. The light has not traveled in a straight line and temporarily offers the ability to see in a curve over the horizon. This has even caused basking walruses to appear from beyond visible range.

Wherever the Earth's relationship with the sun causes our planet to verge on the uninhabitable and immerse us in sensory extremes, so we find great examples of human ingenuity. It is beautiful when these phenomena can be explained, but no less so when they cannot. An Inuit called Aipilik once told of becoming lost after venturing out to retrieve some meat. He was out on the sea ice when a storm blew up. He made a windbreak to sit out the storm and fell asleep. In his dreams he heard a voice telling him that the direction of his camp was to his right, on his lee side. The voice told him that if he headed downwind he would get home. He survived to tell the tale.

CHAPTER 2

The Perfect Illusion: The Sun

He furnishes the world with light and removes
darkness, he obscures and illuminates the rest of the
stars, he regulates in accord with nature's precedent
the changes of the seasons and the continuous rebirth of the year, he dissipates the gloom of heaven
and even calms the storm clouds of the mind of man.

—Pliny the Elder, *Natural History*

The Norse sagas, a sprawling mass of wonderful tales of
North Atlantic life and voyaging, tell the story of Bjarni
Herjólffson. In 986 AD, he set out from Norway to Iceland on a seasonal voyage to meet up with his parents, but when
he arrived he discovered that his father had decided to head off
to Greenland instead. This must have been more than a little bit
irritating, since every crossing of the North Atlantic could be a
Viking's last.

Bjarni decided to follow his father to Greenland. He was
caught in a storm that blew him off course and battled with it for
days before the skies cleared sufficiently for him to catch a
glimpse of the sun. He was able to use it to get his bearings, the

horizon began to make sense again, and he made it safely back to land. During his time at sea he had been blown to the southwest of where he wanted to be and had sighted some distant lands to the west that looked quite inviting. Was he the first European to set eyes on America?

Bjarni's use of the sun allowed him to shape a course and bring news of this sighting back into the Viking fold, where it was woven into the sagas and passed on to us as folklore. There is little doubt that these Viking journeys took place, even if it is hard to be certain of all the details, as archaeological evidence places Nordic settlements on the Newfoundland coastlines at around 1000 AD.

The Vikings undertook extraordinary journeys with the help of the sun, but they are far from the only ones who realized that it could be used to find direction. Most people are familiar with one of the most basic natural navigational ideas employed by our forebears: The sun rises in the east and sets in the west. It is a concept that percolates through popular culture and has done so for millennia, even before the ancient Egyptian sun god Ra descended in the west, sailed through the underworld and then slayed a serpent before being allowed to rise again each morning in the east.

There is of course one small problem with this as a concept. The sun does no such thing. It does not rise; it does not set; it does not move within our solar system at all. How can two fundamental truths be so solid and yet so totally incompatible? As children, we are taught that the Earth revolves around the sun, but our eyes, our culture, our everyday lives seem to demonstrate incontrovertibly that it is the sun that is moving.

To use the sun to find direction effectively it is a good idea to overcome this paradox. It will certainly not be the first time that the heavens have been wrestled with. The history of astronomy catalogs differing ideas meeting at points in history and either getting along very well or exploding apart.

White rabbits and black hats may still materialize at children's parties these days, but otherwise modern illusionists have largely moved on. Their tricks are rarely fully explained. Those who betray such secrets can expect excommunication from the magic community. The author of a book that explained one of nature's greatest illusions should have been grateful that it was not fully published until the year of his death in 1543. Nicolaus Copernicus's *De Revolutionibus Orbium Coelestium Libri VI* (Six Books Concerning the Revolutions of the Celestial Spheres) might have led to his excommunication from a more powerful circle than the magic one had he lived to see his ideas take hold.

The Copernican revolution begins with Copernicus's explanation of how the Earth spins on its axis and orbits around the sun. At the time he was really explaining the greatest of all party tricks: how nature manages to make a fiery ball weighing 330,000 times more than the Earth and burning with a temperature of over 5000°C appear and disappear *without moving*. It is quite a feat of illusion and one that the natural navigator must fully comprehend.

Copernicus was not the first to entertain the idea of a heliocentric model of our solar system, placing the sun rather than the Earth at its center. That honor falls to Aristarchus of Samos around 250 BC, on whose thesis Copernicus built his own. And it was not until some time after Copernicus's death that the revolution in thinking about our solar system really began to take hold. If Copernicus took the first steps from an ancient view of the solar system to a modern one, it was Galileo who played the next major role in this revolution. Galileo is perhaps best described as a fresh pair of eyes, for it was his observations that caused a sensation.

Having made important improvements to the telescope, Galileo used this pioneering piece of technology to observe two key facts that refuted the old view and supported the new. First, he discovered that the surface of the moon was not perfectly smooth. Then he noticed that Jupiter had four orbiting moons of its own. Neither of these facts sound particularly illuminating or controversial today. But the Earth had until then been considered to be both at the center of the universe and surrounded by the perfect heavens. Galileo's observations proved that the moon was not perfect, it had craters and blemishes aplenty, and so could not be part of a perfect heaven. He also showed that if Jupiter had moons orbiting around it then it was behaving as the center of another small part of the universe.

The power of new theories can be proved by the opposition they provoke. The Catholic Church, perhaps receiving its first strong and unwelcome whiff of the power of scientific theory in shaping opinion, began to mobilize against these heretical ideas. Galileo was formally charged by the Inquisition, forced to recant his theories and was kept under house arrest for the rest of his life. If the logic of the Church can be questioned, its tenacity cannot. Pope John Paul II attempted to bring some closure to the matter in 2000, when he issued an apology for Galileo's trial.

The pace of change of celestial understanding did not relent, despite the Church's best efforts. The German astronomer Johannes Kepler realized that the planets orbited elliptically, not in a circle, and Isaac Newton developed the gravitational theory that held all of these observations together. The modern view of the solar system was near complete by Newton's death in 1727.

When trying to understand the role of the sun in ancient journeys, the sources become fewer and the journeys less well known. Herodotus writes about an exploratory voyage commissioned by the ancient Egyptian King Necho II in about 600 BC. Necho II reportedly ordered a Phoenician expedition to sail clockwise around Africa, starting at the Red Sea and returning to the mouth of the Nile. They were gone for three years. Herodotus writes that the Phoenicians, upon returning from their epic expedition, reported that after sailing south and then turning west, they found the sun was on their right, the opposite direction to where they were used to seeing it or expecting it to be. Contemporary astronomical science was simply not strong enough to fabricate such an accurate, fundamental and yet prosaic detail of where the sun would be after sailing past the equator and into the southern hemisphere. It is this that leads many of today's historians to conclude that the journey must have taken place.

Several hundred years later, in about 300 BC, the Mediterranean town of Marseilles was part of the ancient Greek empire and home to an astronomer called Pytheas. He shared with the later explorer Captain James Cook a strong contemporary understanding of the sky and a desire to see more of the planet. An early example of a trend that resurfaces constantly throughout history can be found in Pytheas's travels: Extraordinary journeys often yield pioneering observations and views. Could Darwin have shaken the world so if he had never set foot on the *Beagle* and scrambled tirelessly around distant shores?

Pytheas undertook a journey that added another dimension to the understanding of the relationship between the Earth, the sun, and navigation. Pytheas knew that there was a strong connection between how far north he traveled and the apparent behavior of the sun. He traveled from the Mediterranean to the Arctic, stopping to investigate Britain and Ireland along the way. This was an incredible journey for the time, and his story was not easily swallowed by his peers and later critics, such as the Greek geographer Strabo, who wrote about his exploits more than 200 years later. The irony is that, as with Necho's expedition, it is his extraordinary natural observations, which led to incredulity in his own era, that help us to realize that he really went where he said he did. Pytheas was aware that the length of day would change as he headed north, but some of the extremes he experienced led ancient commentators to raise an eyebrow.

Pytheas pioneered the use of an extremely basic instrument called a gnomon, which does little more than cast a shadow (it is the device found at the center of a sundial). Pytheas knew that the length of the shadow was directly related to how far north he was and the time of year. The farther north he traveled, the longer the sun's shadow grew on average and, importantly, it did so in a predictable and meaningful way.

It is unsurprising that his accounts of a place where a day seemed to last for three months were hard for his Mediterranean peers to take on board. (It is not until the ninth century that such long northern days appear again in literature, when the Irish monk Dicuil wrote of being able to pick the lice from his shirt at midnight.) Pytheas' original account of his voyage has been lost, and so it is impossible to know all his thoughts, but it is unlikely that he would have pushed as far north as he did without reference to those comforting shadows.

Jumping forward over two thousand years to the Second World War, the sun's shadows were being used again. The Long Range Desert Group made a name for themselves by tearing around the Sahara and generally terrifying the usually phlegmatic Germans. They had discovered one of the many foibles of the magnetic compass: its dislike of large lumps of metal, like armored vehicles, and so replaced it with a sun compass, navigating their way with the aid of simple shadows. A thin gnomon stood on a circular plate, which could be adjusted to account for the two key variables: latitude and time. The gnomon's shadow could then be read off the compass plate to reveal direction. Sun compasses were still being issued for use in the desert during the Gulf War in 1990.

The journeys of the Phoenicians, Vikings, Pytheas, and the Long Range Desert Group all help to underline the importance of the relationship between the sun and navigation. But in order for the natural navigator to use it to find direction, it is necessary to unravel and understand the sun's habits.

The Spinning Orb

Passengers on a train look out of the windows and watch the platform "move" backward away from. Relative motion is one of the most deceptive tricks for our eyes, even on a tiny scale such as this. The apparent motion of the sun, its rising and setting, is, as we all now know, due to the Earth spinning. Spin yourself around on an office chair, and you will see the lights on the other side of the room appearing and disappearing from view. If you were then asked whether the lights had actually moved, your answer would be a confident "no."

The Earth spins on its axis once every twenty-four hours. Each part of the globe experiences dawn, day, dusk, and night in turn as the sun comes in and out of view. The Earth also orbits around the sun once every 365 days, creating the year, but there is still a crucial piece to this simple jigsaw that is needed before it can be used by the natural navigator. An explanation is needed for the seasons, a reason why the days are longer in summer than winter and why the sun never rises or sets in exactly the same place from one day to the next.

All of this can be explained by the fact that the Earth's axis of rotation is at an angle relative to its orbit around the sun. This angle is 23½ degrees. This basic mathematical truth delivers the variety in the seasons and explains where on the horizon the sun rises and sets. Understanding this aspect of the Earth–sun relationship is critical to getting to know the direction the sun will be at certain times of day and year, but it is also responsible for some of its more subtle influences.

The diagram opposite brings the words "angle relative to its orbit around the sun" to life. Since the Earth is "tilted" relative to the sun and because it orbits around the sun, it follows that during its annual cycle the amount by which each pole is angled toward the sun varies over the course of the year.

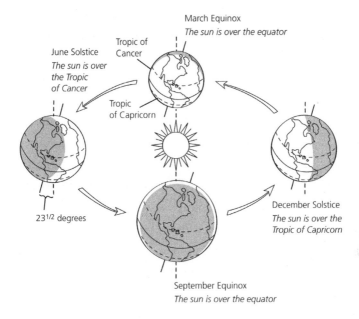

At certain times of the year, the North Pole is tilted toward the sun, and at others it tilts away. At the times that the North Pole is tilting toward the sun, the northern hemisphere is receiving more direct sunlight, and this is summer in the northern hemisphere. The other three seasons can all be traced back to this relationship between angle and orbit. When the Earth moves half an orbit around the sun from a northern hemisphere summer, the season changes from summer to winter. However, after only a quarter of an orbit the northern and southern hemispheres are neither receiving the maximum amount of direct sunlight nor the minimum. This is one of the "in between" seasons, autumn in the northern hemisphere and spring in the southern.

There are four key moments in this orbital cycle. The first is when the North Pole is pointing as much as it possibly can toward the sun. In the northern hemisphere, this is called Mid-summer's Day or the summer solstice, occurring on about June 21 each year, and it is the longest day of the year. A quarter of a year after this, neither pole is pointing toward or away from the sun. It is mid-autumn in the northern hemisphere and this moment is the equinox. It occurs on about September 22 each year. Midwinter's Day in the northern hemisphere or the winter solstice, the shortest day of the year, is on about December 21 each year. Round another quarter turn and there is another moment when once more both poles are perpendicular to the sun's rays, mid-spring in the northern hemisphere and another equinox on about March 20 each year.

The word "equinox" comes from the Latin words meaning "equal" and "night" and on each equinox each place on the globe experiences roughly the same amount of day and night. The words solstice and equinox are familiar to most of us, but their foundation in the simple relationship to that 23½ degree angle is less commonly understood. A knowledge of this angle and where the Earth is in its cycle around the sun makes it possible for the natural navigator to estimate the direction of the sun from anywhere on Earth at any time.

It is also this angle which gives us life on Earth as we know it. If, instead of 23½ degrees, the angle was 0 degrees, there would be no seasons at all. If the angle was too large, then the seasons would be too extreme for most life-forms. Instead, most of the Earth's surface experiences variety within manageable limits, even in Kansas, where Truman Capote wrote about seasons that changed from "ideal apple-eating weather," to "sheep-slaughtering snows" and back to "Indian summer" conditions.

This is the first, but not the last, time that it is necessary to reconcile a mathematical view of the world with a naturally observed one. Natural navigation regularly requires the observer to accommodate both approaches to one particular phenomenon.

A line of latitude is one of the horizontal lines on a globe, all points on which are an equal distance north or south of the Equator. A line of longitude is a line running from the North Pole to the South Pole and is used to define how far east or west a place is from Greenwich.

The Tropics of Cancer and Capricorn, the Arctic and Antarctic Circles and the equator are all more familiar to us as geographical concepts than mathematical ones. These five lines of latitude wrap themselves horizontally around the world and although they have been given names, they would exist even if we did not, because they each reflect one aspect of the Earth–sun relationship.

The sun can only be directly opposite or overhead one spot on earth at any one time. This is true of any two spheres. Think of two billiard balls kissing and then draw them apart. There is still only one spot on each that is nearest the other. It is the combination of the three main attributes of the Earth–sun relationship—the Earth's daily rotation, its 23½ degree "tilt," and its annual orbit around the sun—that explain where this spot on Earth will be.

When the North Pole is tilting towards the sun, it follows that the sun will be overhead a point nearer the North Pole than the South. On the northern hemisphere's summer solstice each year the North Pole is tilted as much as it can be toward the sun, and the sun is directly overhead the most northern point that it can reach on Earth. Over the course of Midsummer's Day this point moves around the Earth, and if it traced a line (think of a magnifying glass burning a moving mark on a globe) then that line would be the Tropic of Cancer. The same theory applies when the South Pole is tilted toward the sun, only this time the sun appears overhead at its most southern extreme. The line in this case is called the Tropic of Capricorn.

The equator is the midway line between the two Tropics. It is where the sun passes overhead in mid-spring and autumn, the two equinox days. The Tropic of Cancer is 23½ degrees north of the equator and the Tropic of Capricorn is 23½ degrees south of it.

The word "tropics" has lost its core meaning. It is not a nebulous word, it means more than hot, humid places with white sand and turquoise waters or perhaps thick rainforests. What the word refers to is a band of the Earth's surface, and the only part where the sun can ever be directly overhead. North of the Tropic of Cancer and south of the Tropic of Capricorn the sun is never directly overhead.

The Arctic and Antarctic Circles are the northern and southern caps where at certain times of year, near the solstices, daylight or night can prevail for long periods. The circles extend 23½ degrees from each pole.

These facts are fundamental to an ability to use the sun to find direction. But they also influence our daily lives. Sometimes this is obvious; patterns of activity reflect the Earth's daily spin and the seasonal orbit around the sun stretches the amount of daylight in summer and makes it warmer, so it is a popular time of year to camp, to travel, to take time off work. It is also the traditional time when livestock reproduce, when crops are grown and then harvested.

Sometimes the relationship requires more lateral thought to unravel. If you head to a busy shopping area, like Fifth Avenue, in midtown Manhattan, in December and feel the crowds bumping into you and making you fractious, it might be worth pausing to contemplate how our shopping habits reflect our planet's journey around the sun. This runs deeper than the fact that bikinis sell well in spring and furry boots in autumn. Consider how the busiest shopping time of year is before Christmas, how Christmas was influenced by Saturnalia, the Roman winter party and the birthday of Mithra, the Iranian god of light, both festivals that celebrated the winter solstice, when the sun stopped moving south and the days stopped shortening. Sol Invictus, the undefeated sun, would soon return and this was something worth celebrating. Some things, like the general mood of midwinter revelry, have changed very little over the centuries.

The Shadow Stick

Two hundred years after Pytheas' voyage toward the land of the midnight sun, the Greek astronomer and mathematician Hipparchus was the first to look at the world as a sphere that could be divided up into 360 degrees. He used Pytheas' shadow measurements to work out the line of latitude that he must have been on and how far north he was at the time of measuring the shadow. A few years later Strabo, the geographer, was then able to look along this line and work out that Pytheas must have been on the north coast of Brittany at the time. The shadow had come of age.

Pytheas' gnomon was a refined form of stick, but any stick will serve the same purpose. There is no better way to tame the sun than by watching shadows move. All that is needed is an open space that will not be disturbed for a day, and a stick. This can be done on a lawn or a beach, in a desert, in snow, or in a parking lot. As we dive deeper into the subject of the sun and where it appears in the sky, it is important to hold on to the idea that there is nothing about the movement of the sun that cannot be understood by putting a stick in the ground and watching its shadow.

Imagine that it is March 21. At dawn, place a stick in the ground and then look to see where the shadow from the sun is cast. Then place a mark at the tip of this shadow. The mark can be anything: chalk, pebble, finger marks in the sand. Wait a while and then look to see where the shadow has moved and put a new mark down at the end of the shadow. Repeat this as regularly as time allows until dusk, and you will have a series of marks. Finally, draw a line that joins these shadow tip marks together and have a good look at it. If you have done a good job you will find a smooth line. The line will be a very shallow curve.

Before analyzing this line, it is worth stopping to think once more about the Earth and the sun. At some point near the middle of the day, the sun will reach its highest point in the sky. It reaches this point at the split second it stops rising and just before it begins to set, which is another way of saying that for one tiny moment each day the sun is neither east nor west of you. At this important instant in each day it is directly above a line that runs from the North Pole, between your feet and on down to the South Pole. It is directly above your meridian or line of longitude. There is an easy way of telling when the sun is at its highest point in the sky and above your line of longitude. It is the moment that it casts its shortest shadow. Wherever you are in the world, the shortest shadow from a stick will always form a perfect north–south line, and it will do this at midday.

Here is a shadow curve from March 21. The shadow gets shorter over the course of the morning and then longer during the afternoon. At midday the shadow is shortest and forms a perfect north–south line:

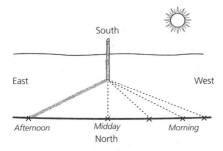

The tips of the shadows are joined to form a gentle curve in March. The shortest shadow will form a perfect north–south line.

It is important next to clarify what midday actually means. For most people it means noon, twelve o' clock, nearly lunch . . . but all these concepts are misleading, messy modern approximations of a precise natural phenomenon. For natural navigators, midday is a literal expression. It means the midpoint of the solar day, the precise moment that is halfway between sunrise and sunset. It does not matter if it is midsummer and the day is eighteen hours long, or a short and bitter seven hours. Midday is the second at which the sun is highest in the sky.

The midday shadow is straightforward, but it does pose one big question: If it is a perfect north–south line, then which is which? The answer lies in that friendly angle of 23½ degrees. The sun is never above a point farther north than the Tropic of Cancer. The

UK, all of Europe, all of the United States, and a lot of other places on the globe are all comfortably north of the Tropic of Cancer, and so for all these places the sun has to be due south at midday, every day of the year. The shortest shadow in these places will always be cast toward the north, the base of the shadow stick forming its southern end. For countries that are south of the Tropic of Capricorn, like New Zealand, the sun will always be due north at midday, and the shadow will point south. In the Tropics it will depend on the time of year: It will either be due north or due south (or conceivably directly overhead), but it will require some thinking about seasons and latitude to work out which.

Dawn and Dusk

Looking to the horizon reveals two very important times for the navigator: the start and end of the day.

The Odyssey, one of the oldest works of Western literature, has had such a deep influence on our culture that scholars tend to drown in their attempts to fully unravel it. Contained within this epic poem is a valuable patchwork of clues to the lives of those who first told and listened to the story. It is a tale about a great sea voyage with many adventures en route on land, and through this we gain an insight into the origins of some important navigational concepts. The relationship between the sun, the horizon, and east and west runs richly through the story.

At one point in his journey, Odysseus is lost and tells his crew that "east and west" mean nothing to them. The historian E. G. R. Taylor has pointed out that the poem mentions that the dawn sun was marking out the direction of east for them. This is probably the earliest extant example of literature highlighting the difference between knowing direction and knowing where you are. Odysseus was able to orient himself using the dawn sun, but this was not much use to him because he had lost track of where he was.

The importance of dawn and dusk for the navigator can be seen by returning to the shadow stick and by considering the idea of putting aside a few minutes each day for a year to mark the points of the shadow tips. That anyone might have the time or the inclination to do this is amusing in a modern context, but this is exactly what the ancients did, at Stonehenge and elsewhere.

The tips joined from one day will make a curve very like those of the day before, but they will be subtly different, and over a year change quite dramatically. You may have guessed already that the two extremes are the summer and winter solstices and the two curves that lie on top of each other and fall in the middle are on the spring and autumn equinoxes. Here are the three lines which delineate the four key moments (the two equinoxes form the same single line) in the annual Earth–sun relationship:

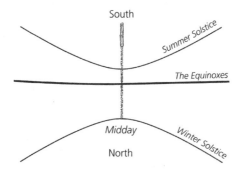

The different shadow tip curves over the course of a year. The shortest shadow forms a perfect north–south line every day of the year.

Why such a dramatic change between midsummer and mid-winter? The answer lies in that 23½ degree angle again. At the summer solstice, the North Pole is inclined towards the sun. What this means to the navigator standing there, metaphorically shivering in the predawn summer cool, chalk clutched in fingers, waiting for a dawn shadow, is that the sun is about to appear somewhere north of east over the horizon. Seventeen or so hours later, the North Pole is still very much tilted toward the sun, and it will set with plenty of north in it, too. The shadow is not a complex beast; it will always fall in the opposite direction of the sun that makes it. After a hard day's marking the ground one look at the June curve will reveal that it has gone from a point southwest of the stick to a point southeast of it.

In December, the South Pole is tilted toward the sun, and so the sun rises and sets with plenty of south in it. At the equinox neither pole is inclined toward the sun, and so it rises due east and sets due west on these days and these lines are very close to straight. (The equinox lines are never perfectly straight except at the equator, because everywhere else on Earth the sun will pass over a point south or north of the observer at midday and cast a shadow in the opposite direction.)

The shadows taken from the stick over a course of a year demonstrate that the popular belief that the sun rises east and sets west is both true and false. It rises due east and sets due west on the two equinoxes, but not on any other day of the year. On the June side of the equinoxes, from northern hemisphere spring to autumn, it will rise and set north of east and on the December side it will rise and set south of east.

The best method for remembering which side of east and west the sun will rise and set is to work back from the seasons. If you are in the northern hemisphere and it is summer, then it follows logically that the North Pole is tilted toward the sun—the sun will rise and set north of east and west. When the South Pole is tilted toward the sun, the sun will rise and set south of east and west.

It was this basic knowledge that gave me a warm confidence in a cold place as I took off in a single engine aircraft from Goose Bay, Newfoundland, in May 2007 to fly solo across the North Atlantic. I had two compasses, three GPS units, and about half a dozen other radio navigation aids to rely upon, but it was the brilliant white glow above a vast dark blue to the northeast that made sense of the direction for me. It is the thing that I remember vividly now, not the dials and screens.

An understanding of the position of the sun at dawn and dusk at different times of the year is key, but there is another vital element in the equation, and that is latitude. How far north or south an observer is does not influence which side of east or west the sun rises and sets, but the amount. At 0 degrees latitude, the equator, the sun will never rise or set more than 23½ degrees from east or west. In the Arctic or Antarctic Circles, there are times when the sun never sets or rises, because its rising and setting points have moved so far north or south that they have met again.

Most North Americans live in the northern temperate zone, in latitudes between the Tropic of Cancer and the Arctic Circle. The effect of the sun at either end of the day is therefore less dramatic than in the Arctic and much more so than at the equator. For example, in Vancouver the sun will rise close to northeast and set close to northwest on Midsummer's Day. On Midwinter's

Day it will be close to southeast and southwest. The difference between midsummer and midwinter's sunrise direction is about 90 degrees—huge. Farther north than Vancouver the difference grows even wider, farther south it shrinks.

Although you can have complete certainty on two days of the year, the equinoxes, there is no natural method for determining exactly where the sun will rise and set. This comes from local knowledge and experience. When you have lived in the same place for a year, even in a city center, casual observation can teach you where to expect to see the dawn sun. In an unknown area, it is possible to estimate the approximate bearing of sunrise from a knowledge of latitude and season, but to fix it more precisely it is necessary to cross-refer with other clues, like the stars.

The word "solstice" derives from the Latin words "*sol*" and "*sistere*," the "sun" and "standing still." If one makes a study of the shift in position of each day's sunrise, the sun appears to move gradually along the horizon, but it does not do so at a uniform pace. Although the Earth orbits around the sun at a fairly constant rate, the point of sunrise races through due east at the equinoxes and then decelerates at each solstice until it appears to almost stop. Think of a ball bouncing horizontally between two springs along the horizon: It accelerates to its fastest near the middle but comes to a "standstill" at each end before accelerating back again. This effect is everywhere, you can even see it in a photo of a merry-go-round: The faces of people in the middle of the picture are blurred but on either side of the picture they are crisper. The people are all moving at the same speed, yet some appear to have stopped, and others are whizzing by.

Approximate sunrise directions from Britain

NE	E	SE
Midsummer's day	The Equinoxes	Midwinter's day
June	March and September	December

The direction of sunrise and sunset changes more each day near the equinoxes than it does near the solstices.

The sun's movement along the horizon on the days either side of each solstice is very small compared to that at each equinox. Bringing this down to earth, the shadow curves change most rapidly in spring and autumn and hover around the same shape at the solstices.

There is sometimes a temptation to think that this is all a remarkable coincidence. It is extraordinary that the sun should happen to sit neatly on certain lines, like north or south, at certain times, or that it should happen to rise exactly east or set west at others. It is, however, a false temptation, because the cardinal directions and the motion of celestial objects, including the sun, are just different ways of looking at the same thing. Our world has been divided up into four principal directions and given the labels north, south, east, and west because these are the labels that best reflect the way the objects we see in the sky appear to us to behave.

In this sense, when we say "I will head south," we are saying that we will head toward the sun at midday, not because that is how we will find the direction, but because that is what it means at its purest. We have stripped away any conventions, any thoughts of compasses or even maps. East is not concerned with Asia or chopsticks, Confucius or Moscow. Eastern means the direction that the sun will rise on the equinoxes and everything else is window dressing on the largest of windows.

The ancients understood this in a way that modern minds find more difficult to comprehend. The Greek word for north was *arctos*, which means "bear." The northern constellation was the Bear. The direction and the object in the sky were not just synonymous, but identical. Although they had beliefs encapsulated in myth, the Greeks did not have a true picture of what lay in the far north. They did not have photographs of snow-swept wastes and wild landscapes, which meant that their concept of north was left in a purer state.

To understand the relationship between nature and direction at its purest and most fundamental level, the modern mind needs to be refreshed and to move away from the conventional ideas and imagery of direction. The natural navigator needs to restore the relationship between direction and the sky to its former loftier status, where direction is not simply found by looking to the sky but actually *is* what is seen in the sky.

The Sun's Arc

Knowing the sun, understanding where it is and where it has been over the hours, days, and year, is important even when it cannot be seen directly. The sun leaves great big footprints that can be read even when it is smothered in cloud, even at night. Most of the techniques that work on land can be read with more confidence and authority when the navigator has a familiarity with the sun's arc. Mosses on the north side of trees and buildings retreat and shrivel in summer as they dry in the morning and evening sunlight.

The direction and behavior of the sun at sunrise, midday, and sunset can be divined from an understanding of the shadow stick, which also demonstrates that the sun does not jump from any one point in the sky to another. It does not jump anywhere, but traces a smooth arc across the sky. By putting these facts together it becomes possible to do some direction finding. What direction will the sun be in the middle of the afternoon in Vancouver in September? The answer to that question can be found without any tricks, but by returning to the key points in the Earth–sun relationship.

September is halfway between midsummer and midwinter—it is the month of an equinox. This means that the sun will rise close to due east and set close to due west everywhere in the world. It will be due south at midday in the UK, as the UK is north of the Tropic of Cancer. The middle of the afternoon is halfway from midday to sunset and so the sun will have moved approximately halfway from south to west. The sun will be close to southwest.

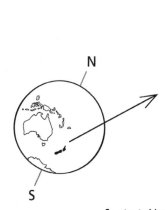

Sunrise in New Zealand in June.

What direction will the sun be one hour after sunrise in New Zealand in June? Although south of the equator and slightly closer to it, New Zealand's latitude is comparable to that of Vancouver. It is close to the June solstice, which means that the North Pole is tilted toward the sun. There will be a lot of north in the sunrise direction. New Zealand is south of the Tropic of Capricorn, so at midday the sun will have reached due north. One hour is only a small fraction of its journey from sunrise to midday so a good estimate would be that it will be just north of northeast.

This is where the art begins, and with practice it is possible to become very good at reading the sun in this way. There are different ways of honing your skills: You can compare your estimate with a compass or guess an exact bearing for a time and place, and then look up the answer in a book or on the Internet. Or you may choose not to translate the direction into any modern concept at all, but simply relate it to what you see in front of you as you travel.

The simple ideas can become more complex. In March, a walk to work toward the sun at sunrise will then require walking home toward the sun again at sunset. . . . This will retrace the same steps—out east, back west. In December in Vancouver, a walk with the sun on your back at sunrise will require a walk with it over your right shoulder to find your way back at sunset—out northwest, back southeast. Thinking of your own examples will help bring the different pieces together. As a rule of thumb, things are more straightforward nearer the equinoxes and become more involved closer to the solstices.

When on a navigational research trip to the Libyan Sahara, I was fortunate that it was early March, not too far from the spring equinox. The sun was ferocious near the middle of the day, but it was always there to be found, and it broke the horizon predictably close to east and west, a few degrees to the south of them. It was possible for me to walk for hours, using my own shadow as a compass.

So much of reading the sun for direction comes down to the art of interpolation. The better the sun's arc is known, the better this art can be practiced. There is another important aspect to how the sun moves, how it traces its arc, and how this relates to its change in bearing over the course of a day, which must be added to the equation.

The sun's rate of movement is perfectly simple. It moves across the sky at a uniform speed: 15 degrees per hour. This is the relative speed that nearly all celestial objects move when viewed from Earth, because it completes one full revolution every twenty-four hours. The equation is simply 360 degrees divided by 24 equals 15. So 15 degrees is just a mathematical way of saying one twenty-fourth of a circle.

It is however a more complex concept than this equation might suggest. The sun is moving at 15 degrees per hour, but it is not usually moving parallel to the horizon. The sun is moving across the sky at a constant speed, but the change in its bearing is unfortunately not constant. An analogy would be when climbing a mountain, even if the gradient does not tire the walker at all and they move their feet at the same speed, their speed in any one direction will vary depending on the angle of the slope. The extreme example that illustrates this point is that when climbing a steep face the climber would hardly be moving horizontally across the ground at all, even if moving over the surface at the same pace.

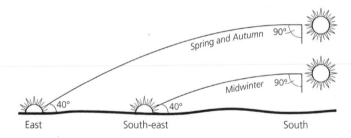

The sun moves at a steeper angle at the start and end of the day than it does in the middle of the day. This is how it appears from Vancouver.

The sun also climbs mountains and walks on nice flat plains. At midday it is always, for a fraction of a second, moving horizontally, but it starts and finishes the day at a steeper angle, which is related to the latitude of the observer (it is in fact close to a number called the "colatitude," is 90 degrees minus the observer's latitude). At the poles, the sun moves horizontally, either above or below the horizon. At the equator, the sun rises and sets vertically. In Vancouver it will rise at an angle close to 40 degrees, because the latitude is close to 50 degrees, but in northern Scotland it will rise at an angle closer to 30 degrees because the latitude there is closer to 60 degrees.

What does this mean for direction finding? The higher the observer's latitude, the closer the sun is to moving horizontally, and so the more regularly the bearing of the sun will alter. At the poles it will move around the horizon at exactly 15 degrees per hour, but at the equator the sun can rise due east, pass directly overhead, and set due west—in that situation the sun changes bearing by 180 degrees in a second at midday, from due east to due west. That is a rare and extreme example, but it goes to show that understanding the arc is important in knowing how reliable your estimate might be. In practice what this means is that finding direction from the sun in the Tropics is a lot harder than at higher latitudes.

Difficult Times

In ancient times, the sun was so crucial to navigation that problems arose when it was obscured. As St. Paul the Apostle recounts, "And when neither sun nor stars in many days appeared, and no small tempest lay on us, all hope that we should be saved was then taken away."

When the sun is hidden by cloud it is still shining as brightly and its light is still reaching the ground, otherwise it would be night, but the rays of sunlight are diffused, bounced around in the cloud and then finally released down to earth. However, they do still come from the same source direction, and there is a straightforward method of looking for this. The trick is to use a long thin blade; it can be of a knife, paper, bark or leaf. If you twist the blade in a place that is open to light from all parts of the sky, you can often detect a fan-shaped shadow, which narrows to a line as you twist the blade and then grows to a fan again. The blade will point to the sun behind the clouds when the shadow is skinniest, when it is closest to a line.

The only thing to be wary of when using this method is that it will only tell you where the brightest part of the sky is. If you have an even spread of overcast skies, then this will likely be where the sun is, but if the sky is uneven it can be misleading. Under an opening in a wood, for example, you will only discover where the opening is, and if it is only partially overcast then the sun can bounce off cloud edges and bamboozle.

The sun was vital for Bjarni Herjólffson. Part of the reason for this was that he sailed at high latitudes and was a seasonal voyager. The Vikings went to sea in summer, and the high latitudes gave extremely long days, so the stars were of very limited use. But they would also often have encountered cloud cover and sea fogs. The writer and navigator Leif Karlsen is one of many who believe that the Vikings pioneered an unusual method for finding the sun in adverse conditions, called the *solarsteinn*, or sunstone. The sunstone, which was composed of Icelandic spar crystals, would have worked by its ability to polarize the light, making the true direction of the sun possible to detect by comparing the light and dark patterns from a variety of directions. Karlsen suggests that this method could have been used to find the direction of the sun, even when it was below the horizon. He points to hints in Norse myth and in the writings of King Olav: "A stone with which one could see where the sun was in heaven."

One Viking tale tells of a farmer's son, Sigurd, who boasted of being able to see the sun when others could not. King Olav the Stout put him to the test on a day that was overcast and snowing and he triumphed. Had he used a simple blade or perhaps something more unique, a sunstone? If so, this would qualify as one of the earliest navigational instruments.

The sun is behind so many natural phenomena that understanding how it behaves yields clues to the behavior of a plethora of other things, from ants to humans, huge old oak trees to puddles and lichen. Let's take a final look at the sun's arc in action, and how shadows from simple gnomons—whether they are sticks, trees or knives—can help a navigator find direction.

Hidden Tales

Very few people these days spot the clues to the sun's presence that can be found all around us. With practice, the outdoors can be read like a series of short stories about the sun's daily arc and annual journey.

The yews of Kingley Vale, a mysterious and ancient reserve in southern England, claim among their kind some that are 2,000 years old. They drew me there one bracing December afternoon. It was during a cold snap, a winter high pressure system that let the heat out by night and then failed to top it up sufficiently by day. The sun was setting in the southwest; it had finished its shift. There was frost in places, but not everywhere; the sun had done its best over the short day. I watched some small boys smashing large sticks into the inch-thick pond ice.

The Kingley Vale yews are arranged in tight sinewy clumps, broad at the base and then curving more than tapering up to a distinct peak. On one side of the largest clump there was a clear frost shadow, broad at its base and moving out to a rounded edge farthest from the trees. The yews had been kind enough to play fat shadow stick for me. In the middle of the day, the sun had thawed the frost that it could reach, but could not reach the ground on the northern side of the yews. The line from the center of the trees to the curved edge of the frost was a perfect south-to-north line. The trees had helped to create this frost compass, but this was not about the trees. It was about the sun.

In the Alps, the same sun warms the glaciers, causing the ice to melt, but it cannot reach every inch of the cold ground. In a few places a large boulder might act as a heavy parasol. The ice

GLACIER TABLES.

all around the stone melts away and it is left standing on a column of ice, proud and high. Eventually the sun will reach below the boulder and begin to melt the ice pillar, but it will not do it evenly. The sun's arc is to the south and so the southern side of the pillar receives more warming sunlight. The southern ice trickles away, and the rock begins to tip and slip slowly down toward the south, dipping its southern edge, bowing in deference to the southern arc of the sun.

Finding direction by using the sun is helped enormously by familiarity with some of the angles and knowledge of the earth's orbit, but it remains a natural clue that can be befriended in any open space. Placing a stick in the ground and spending a few minutes observing shadows will reveal everything you could ever need to know about the sun's arc. You will begin to notice subtle patterns and beautiful symmetries.

The next time you spend a day at the seaside, plant your stick. If you join the mark from two shadows of equal length in a straight line it will form a perfect east–west line. A coincidence? No, two shadows of equal length are just two moments equal in time either side of midday. It is geometry, which is another way of saying we have brought the sun down to lines in the sand.

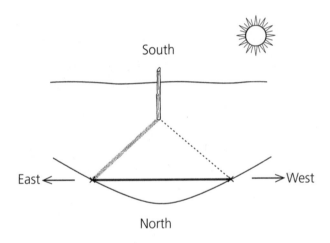

The tips of two shadows of equal length joined together make a perfect east–west line.

CHAPTER 3

The Firmament

I n the South Atlantic ocean, squid fishermen use metal halide lamps to lure the squid to their nets. The lamps can be seen from space and burn more brightly than the light from the vast cities of Buenos Aires and Rio de Janeiro.

Popular understanding of the night sky has been slipping away since Thomas Edison's invention of the electric lightbulb toward the end of the nineteenth century. Light pollution has obscured the stars from our view of the world and, consequently, our minds. This has severed a relationship with a part of nature that has featured strongly in human history. It is tempting to assume that this trend is limited to industrialized Western society, but there are indigenous desert people who can no longer name a star. They might not live in towns, own computers, or have access to GPS, but they use generators and electric lighting. I was once asked by a Tuareg man in the Sahara to show him how to find the direction of Mecca by using the stars. He could point toward Mecca using landmarks and the sun, but told me in a pained mixture of French, English, Arabic, and Tuareg that his father knew how to read the night sky, but he did not.

Despite this erosion of popular knowledge, the desire to understand the night sky has not disappeared. It is rare to come across someone who professes to have no interest in the stars at all, and learning to use the stars to find direction is an elegant way of reconnecting with the night sky.

The stars appear in literature from the outset, and their use in navigation must pre-date language itself. Odysseus stayed awake on his boat at night, holding his course by watching the Pleiades or Seven Sisters, and the constellation of Boötes, and by keeping the Great Bear on his left. In the Bible we are told who made the stars and how they are arranged according to direction. There are references to the celestial sphere in Buddhist literature and the Quran, which explains that stars can guide in the darkness of land and sea. For thousands of years, the stars were the objects that unified the human journey, metaphorically, philosophically, and practically.

The Phoenicians, Greeks, Vikings, Polynesians, Chinese, Arabs, Inuit, and many other peoples throughout the history of humankind understood the relationship between the stars and direction. There are Anglo-Saxon references to the "*lad steorra*" or leading star dating back to the ninth century. More recently, an understanding of how to use the stars was viewed as a mark of sophistication and worldliness. In his 1883 book *33 Years Among Our Wild Indians*, Colonel Richard Dodge noted, in a way that might cause riots if published today, "I have never yet seen an

Indian who had mounted the ladder of human progress suffi-ciently far to have observed that there is one star which never perceptibly changes its place."

The fact that so few people today are able to point out the North Star in the night sky proves that its place in popular aware-ness is not dictated by a mounting of "the ladder of human prog-ress," but rather by cultural priorities and necessity.

While popular understanding of the stars has diminished, there have been huge advances within academic circles over the centu-ries. Astronomical knowledge marched on through history with different civilizations acting as custodians, but the ancients proved that an ability to use the stars to find direction need not be tied to a scientific understanding of the universe. Simplicity is key.

The ancient Greek view of the universe was simple, beautiful, and very practical. It survives to this day—surprising, considering that there are not a lot of concepts that have passed through the Middle Ages, the Renaissance, the Enlightenment, and the Indus-trial Revolution to emerge intact. The celestial sphere was and remains a great way of understanding the night sky.

The Celestial Sphere

The human need to explain what we see has always been strong, but the methods we employ to do so have changed dramati-cally. The Western approach is now dominated by the empirical method and relies primarily upon observation and experiment rather than theory. This approach to the development of knowl-edge represents the great divide between myth and science. But throughout history, humankind can be seen to have been striving to answer the same questions. Some may claim that the mathematics of gravitational singularity or the Big Bang Theory provide no clearer explanation as to why we are here than the Venezuelan myths of the evening star chasing the other stars and forcing them to climb trees and gather fruit.

In ancient Greece, myth had an important place in contemporary thought, but it coexisted in perfect harmony with a growing theoretical interest in the physical world. In around 600 BC the philosopher Thales of Miletus attempted to explain the world in terms of water. He saw the world as a disc that floated on a huge ocean. The fact that his explanation was wrong is far less important than the fact that he was attempting a physical explanation for the world around him. The myths were not intended to be understood literally in the way that Thales' theory was, and so he can be seen as helping to forge a path between myth and science. His theory has been disproved. The myths remain. What also endures from the time of ancient Greece is the concept of the night sky as a celestial sphere encircling the Earth. While this has been disproved in purely physical terms, it lives on as the most effective way of conceptualizing what we are able to observe in the skies above us.

The appearance of the night sky is dominated by certain key features and relationships. There are approximately 6,000 stars visible to the naked eye in ideal conditions, of which only about 2,500 are visible at any one time. After taking time to observe them the following characteristics become apparent.

The first thing that strikes most observers are the patterns of stars in the sky, or the constellations. Critically, these patterns remain constant; the constellations do not noticeably change shape—from this we came to realize that the stars are fixed in position relative to each other.

The second important observation is that, although the stars appear stationary relative to each other, they are not stationary relative to the horizon. Their movement is slow and varies in direction depending on the location of an observer and the direction in which they are looking, but some general principles apply. The stars rise in the east and in the west they set. In the northern hemisphere, there is a star in the north that appears not to move, while other stars close to it wheel around it in a counterclockwise direction without rising or setting. In the southern hemisphere the stars wheel clockwise about a point above the southern horizon, but there is no star there to fix this point.

The next thing to note is that the stars appear to rise and set in exactly the same spots on the horizon every single night. If Sirius rises in a valley between two peaks and sets behind a certain tree one night, then it will always be seen to rise and set at those same points if observed from the same place.

The final critical piece of the puzzle is that at different times of the year, different stars and constellations are visible. Scorpius is best viewed in June and Orion in December. Over many nights of observation, the reason for this becomes evident: The stars appear to rise four minutes earlier each evening. The cycle comes back to its starting point each year, since 365 lots of four minutes makes twenty-four hours.

These attributes were noted by the ancient Greeks and helped to shape their view of the heavens, a view that has become known as the celestial sphere.

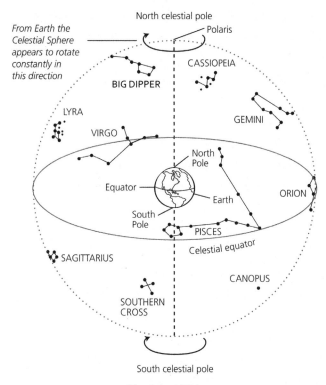

North celestial pole

Polaris

*From Earth the
Celestial Sphere
appears to rotate
constantly in
this direction*

CASSIOPEIA

BIG DIPPER

LYRA

GEMINI

VIRGO

North
Pole

Equator

Earth

ORION

South
Pole

PISCES

Celestial equator

SAGITTARIUS

CANOPUS

SOUTHERN
CROSS

South celestial pole

The Celestial Sphere.

All of these observations and a lot more can be explained by returning to an Earth-centric rather than heliocentric view of the universe and thinking of the Earth as being surrounded by a gigantic glass sphere. On the inside of this giant orb are painted 6,000 stars, some brighter than others. The sphere itself is attached to the earth by an imaginary pole that runs right through the Earth's North and South Poles.

Although this is now only a model, a mental picture to enable us to conceptualize what is happening, to the ancients it was real. In the National Archaeological Museum of Naples there is a marble statue that dates from about the second century. It shows the figure of Atlas heavily weighed down by a sphere on his shoulders. The sphere in this case is not Earth but a depiction of the heavens, complete with constellations. It represents a physical crystallization of the way in which the Greeks saw the universe and which has endured to this day.

The geography of the celestial sphere mirrors that of Earth. The points where the imaginary pole touches the sphere are called the north and south celestial poles. They are directly above the North and South Poles. The line on the sphere that lies above the Earth's equator is called the celestial equator and, as on Earth, it divides the sphere in half. The sphere also has its own versions of latitude and longitude, called declination and Greenwich Hour Angle (GHA) respectively. For the purposes of natural navigation, celestial longitude or GHA is not relevant, but celestial latitude or declination is.

Wherever you are in the world, you will be surrounded by a horizon on all sides. The sky that envelops someone looking up from Earth appears as a dome. It never changes shape, even as the objects that spread over the dome can be seen to move across it. The dome that can be seen is always one half of the celestial sphere. Its midpoint will be the point directly over your head, a point that is known as your zenith.

Imagine that you are in a boat in the middle of a calm ocean with perfect horizons all around you. The angle from the horizon to your zenith will be 90 degrees, whichever direction you look. If you look up from one horizon all the way to your zenith and then, turning round so that you do not fall over, follow the same line down to the opposite horizon, you will have looked along a full 180 degrees of the sky, one half of a circle—the half of the celestial sphere that is visible to you at that moment.

The stars appear to move, because the celestial sphere is in constant steady motion. In the celestial sphere view of the night sky, the Earth remains still, and the sphere rotates around it once every twenty-three hours and fifty-six minutes. The sphere rotates clockwise when viewed from vertically above the north celestial pole.

Understanding where you are on Earth and therefore which part of the celestial sphere you are looking at, combined with knowledge of the rotation of the sphere around the poles, will allow you to use stars to navigate naturally. This is true even if you do not know the names of the stars themselves. Once you have grasped the few fundamental concepts, you will discover how to bring the night sky to life in a meaningful way, and this will remain with you forever.

It is perhaps easiest to understand the motion of the stars by looking first at the extremes. At the North Pole, the point directly overhead, the zenith, is the north celestial pole, and only the northern half of the celestial sphere can be seen. The stars in the southern half will never rise above the horizon and become visible. This is because the sphere is rotating about the poles, the stars never move relative to each other, and so stars south of the celestial equator can never climb higher than the horizon from the North Pole.

From the North Pole, the stars near the horizon appear to move horizontally from left to right, revolving counterclockwise higher in the sky and around Polaris, or the North Star, directly overhead. The stars are slowly circling, some forming large circles along the horizon, shrinking to smaller and smaller ones closer to the North Star, which sits at the north celestial pole itself and does not appear to move at all.

The experience would be nearly identical at the South Pole, only there the stars move the other way, from right to left near the horizon and clockwise overhead. At the equator, the visible half of the celestial sphere will change constantly, with new stars rising vertically over the eastern horizon and setting vertically below the western one.

North America lies between the equator and the North Pole, and so from here the night sky moves in a way that sits between each extreme. Some stars rise and set, but other stars near the north celestial pole never rise nor set: They rotate counterclockwise around the North Star.

The way the stars move relative to the horizon will be determined by the observer's latitude and the apparent motion of the sphere. If your latitude is 55° north, then you are 35° south of the North Pole, which has a latitude of 90°. Your horizons have shifted by 35° from the North Pole. It would be possible to see some southern stars, in theory stars that are 35° south of the celestial equator. The night sky is scrupulously fair and evenhanded, however, and if it gives you a chance to see more of the southern stars at times, then you will lose sight of some of the northern stars at times, too.

The critical thing to keep in mind is that the sphere is revolving around the celestial poles at all times, wherever you are on Earth. The north and south celestial poles are the only two spots on the sphere that do not appear to move. An observer's latitude determines both which celestial pole can be seen and how high it will be in the sky. Standing at the North Pole, the north celestial pole is directly overhead, but standing at the equator you are halfway between each pole, and the two celestial poles, will sit motionless on your north and south horizons respectively.

At a latitude of 55° north, the north celestial pole will appear lower than overhead, but higher than the horizon—55° higher, to be precise. You can see some stars rise and set in the east and west, but near the celestial pole they will wheel counterclockwise around that spot in the sky. Over the southern horizon, the stars will trace a shallow arc, still rising in the east and setting in the west, but moving in a gentle arc from left to right.

The celestial sphere can appear complicated initially, but it is worth investing time in because it can help to make sense of observations without any tricks or the need to memorize the names of stars. It becomes possible to make your own deductions and discoveries, and this is where a lot of the satisfaction of using the stars at night is to be found.

Once the sphere has been befriended, it is possible to lie on a beach in a foreign country and make sense of a group of stars in the night sky that you do not recognize. After half an hour you might notice that they have moved slightly, and your understanding of the celestial sphere will make it possible to deduce the direction of an unknown constellation, seen from a new part of the world for the first time.

The Celestial Poles

If an object in the night sky sits directly over your destination, you can be sure that it will point you in the right direction, even when you cannot see your destination, even when it is thousands of miles away. Imagine that you have arranged to meet someone under a tall solitary streetlight at the far end of a long road that runs over the top of a hill. You would see the light long before you could see the person you were meeting, and you would know the direction they were situated before you could see them. If you can find a star over your destination, it will act as the best possible light to show the way, visible from quarter of the globe away. Imagine calling a friend several thousand miles away and asking them to tell you the name of the star directly overhead, then finding that star on your horizon and setting off toward it. The celestial sphere would continue to turn after you had set off, so you would need to regularly call for a new star to follow. There are, however, two points in the night sky that do not move.

The celestial poles are invaluable for using the stars to find direction, because they are points in the night sky that sit directly and permanently over the North and South Poles. Even if you are in the Tropics and only need to travel a few miles, if you are heading north, you are still looking for a way to travel toward the North Pole.

Stars can do more than indicate one single direction; they can be used to find a series of different directions that demonstrate the shortest possible route for getting to the point below them. The shortest route between two points is very rarely a straight line, since the Earth is spherical. The quickest way from A to B over a sphere is a curve over the surface, a line that is called a great circle. Over short distances this does not usually make a significant difference, but it becomes important if you are traveling over long distances, such as crossing an ocean. This is the reason that the flight paths on long-haul flights often show a curve. By following a star you are taking the best possible curved path toward the point beneath it, something that is very hard to achieve using a compass.

The North Star

As we have seen, there is a prominent star in the night sky which sits very close to the north celestial pole and is known as Polaris, or the North Star. It is a highly visible star, but not the brightest, which is a very common misconception. Polaris features so vividly in our cultural history of the night sky that this is often mistaken for true brightness. Literary references to the North Star abound. It appears in Shakespeare in both *A Midsummer Night's Dream* and *Julius Caesar*:

> But I am constant as the northern star,
> Of whose true fix'd and resting quality
> There is no fellow in the firmament

> —*Julius Caesar* (3.1, 60–2)

Wordsworth refers to it thus, in *The Excursion*:

> Chaldaean shepherds, ranging trackless fields,
> Beneath the concave of unclouded skies
> Spread like the sea, in boundless solitude,
> Looked on the polar star, as on a guide
> And guardian of their course, that never closed
> His steadfast eye.

As Shakespeare and Wordsworth make clear, the reason for the prominence of Polaris in our thinking is its steadfastness, not its brightness. While all other objects in the night sky appear to move across or around in the sky, Polaris does not.

On a clear night in the northern hemisphere there is a simple method for finding the North Star, using a group of seven stars called the Big Dipper (also known as the "Plough" or "Saucepan"). The method is as follows:

Find the Big Dipper. This large group of seven stars is very easily recognized in the northern half of the sky, both from its distinctive shape and because each of its stars are bright. Its shape never changes, although it can appear on its side or even upside down.

Next, identify the two "pointer stars." These are the stars that a liquid would run off if you tipped up the "saucepan." Now visually gauge the distance between the pointer stars and look along the pointer stars to a point in the sky five times that distance beyond them. The star on its own in that part of the sky is the North Star. The point on the horizon directly below that star is due north.

Polaris is known to almost all northern hemisphere cultures. It was Grahadhara in Northern India and Yilduz in Turkey. It has been known as al-Qiblah to the Arabs, in testament to its aid in

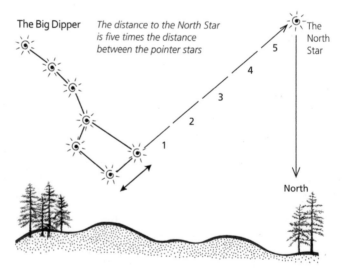

Using the Big Dipper to find Polaris, the North Star.

finding the direction of Mecca, and the Chinese had at least four names for it, over hundreds of years.

Yet for all its cultural luminescence, it is only the forty-eighth brightest star in the sky. It stands out because it is the brightest star in its patch of the sky. If you see two stars of similar brightness close to each other you cannot be looking at the North Star, which always appears to be the only one of comparable brightness in its immediate vicinity.

Polaris is less than a degree away from the celestial pole, meaning that it will always give a clear indication of north. A vertical line dropped down from Polaris to the horizon will be within 1 degree of true north. It is possible to make this line to the horizon accurately by hanging a weight on a string and then suspending it from your thumb with your thumbnail touching Polaris. This method can bring you closer to true north than many people will manage to get even with a good compass or the help of GPS. (Compasses can be used to find magnetic north, but an adjustment to this needs to be made to find true north—the direction of the North Pole. Compasses are also always susceptible to deviation from nearby metal. GPS is excellent at working out position, but less strong at finding direction.)

Using the Big Dipper method is the easiest way of finding the North Star and the reason it works so well can be seen in the celestial sphere. The Big Dipper is close enough to the north celestial pole that it wheels around the North Star, never setting for those in northern latitudes. Stars that behave like this are called circumpolar stars.

The Big Dipper is what is called an asterism, which means that while it is a shape that is recognized in the sky, it is not actually

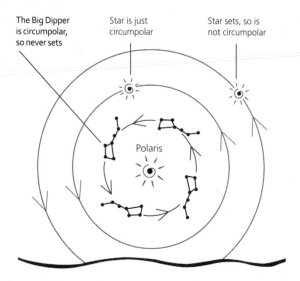

The Big Dipper is circumpolar, so never sets

Star is just circumpolar

Star sets, so is not circumpolar

Polaris

Looking north in the northern hemisphere, the stars rotate counterclockwise around Polaris, the North Star.

one of the eighty-eight formally recognized constellations. It is in fact part of the constellation of Ursa Major, or the Great Bear. This was the constellation that Odysseus was keeping on his left as he sailed east from Calypso's island.

The Big Dipper can be used to find Polaris because it helps organize the sky around a familiar shape. It acts as a signpost, confirming that you are looking at a northern part of the celestial sphere and pointing the way toward the north celestial pole. Although the Big Dipper method is the most straightforward, there are many ways of finding north. All that is needed is some familiarity with the northern half of the celestial sphere, which then acts as a map, and once one feature has been recognized it helps point the way to another recognizable one. In this way it is possible in the northern hemisphere to find the North Star from any point in the night sky.

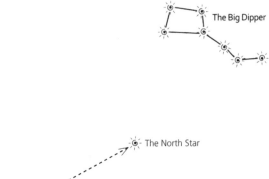

Using Cassiopeia to find Polaris, the North Star.

The constellation of Cassiopeia is also easy to find and lies on the opposite side of the celestial pole from the Big Dipper, making it a good second option at times when the Big Dipper is obscured or very low in the sky. Cassiopeia looks like a slightly stretched "W" in the sky. Like all circumpolar stars it wheels around the pole and can be found on its side or upside down, as an "M." Having found Cassiopeia, the next thing to do is imagine a flat tray lying across the top of the "W." Now imagine a line that runs at right angles to this tray away from the top left of the "W" and double the width of the tray. This line will take you very close to the North Star.

Once you understand the celestial sphere, it is possible to invent your own methods for finding Polaris. Never be intimidated by the names of stars or constellations; there is no such thing as the "right" name. There are only conventions, and if the conventions do not work for you then ignore them and invent your own. Americans think of a Big Dipper, where Brits see a "Plough." The Inuit call it "Tukturjuit," the Caribou. The Aztecs personified the Big Dipper as the destructive god Tezcatlipoca, whose tricks included disguising himself as a jaguar, wizardry, and generally leading the virtuous astray.

The only ingredient missing in describing the location of Polaris in the sky is its elevation, its angle above the horizon. This is where the symmetry and beauty of the sphere really comes into play. At the North Pole, the latitude is 90° north, and Polaris appears overhead, 90° above the horizon. At the equator, the latitude is 0 degrees, and Polaris is sitting on the horizon, 0 degrees above it. This direct relationship applies whatever the latitude, anywhere on Earth. The north celestial pole, indicated by Polaris, will be exactly the same angle above the horizon that an observer is north of the equator. Berlin is 22 degrees farther north than Cairo, and so the north celestial pole and Polaris will be 22 degrees higher in the sky in Berlin than it will be in Cairo.

The Southern Stars

In the southern hemisphere it is the south celestial pole that needs to be found, but there is not a prominent star close to the south celestial pole, which makes searching for it a little more complex than looking for Polaris in the north.

The Southern Cross is a constellation that is almost as familiar to northern ears, if not eyes, as the North Star. In ancient times, it was not an independent constellation. Instead, it formed part of the Centaur, but the ancients would have been familiar with its stars. Pliny the Elder and Hipparchus both alluded to them. It was hived off from the Centaur to become a separate constellation at some point in the sixteenth century.

This is only the European perspective. The stars of the Southern Cross would have been familiar to Aboriginal and other southern cultures for as long as people have been looking to the heavens. The indigenous tribes of the Kalahari Desert, for example, see the eyes of a giraffe in the Southern Cross.

The Southern Cross is best thought of as having four stars, although there is a fifth present. At the head of the cross is the red giant, Gacrux, and at the foot is the blue-white Acrux. The south celestial pole lies four and a half times the distance from Gacrux to Acrux in the same direction beyond the Southern Cross.

It is good practice to look for the two trailing stars, Hadar and Rigil Kent, known as the "pointers," to confirm that you have the

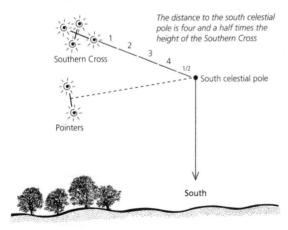

The distance to the south celestial pole is four and a half times the height of the Southern Cross

Using the Southern Cross and the Pointers to find the south celestial pole.

right part of the sky and to make sure you have the true Southern Cross, not another group of four stars like the nearby "False Cross." As the Southern Cross wheels clockwise around the pole, these two very bright stars, which still form part of the constellation of the Centaur, follow it. If you join the two "pointers" together and then take a line that bisects them this line will also run to the south celestial pole. The intersection of the lines from the Southern Cross and this bisection gives a fixed point in the sky. It is not as neat a solution as finding Polaris, but it does work.

Rising and Setting Stars

One of the cornerstones of observing the stars and using them to find direction is the fact that they rise and set in exactly the same place when viewed from the same location, since the sphere continues to turn in a regular way and the stars are fixed in position on the sphere. At certain times of year the stars may be blotted out by the sun's light, but they are still rising and setting in the same places, even when invisible.

If a star is north of the celestial equator then it will always rise and set north of east and west and if south of the celestial equator then it will always rise and set south of east and west.

If the northern stars rise and set north and the southern stars rise and set south, then there must be some stars that lie in between. The celestial equator, the line on the celestial sphere that runs above the Earth's equator, intersects the horizon at two points for all observers: due east and due west. This is the case wherever you are on the planet. If a constellation can be found that lies on or very close to the celestial equator, then it follows that it must rise and set east and west. And one of the brightest and easiest to recognize constellations does indeed straddle the celestial equator: Orion, or the Hunter, a constellation that has been seen by pretty much everyone who has ever looked at the night sky.

Orion contains within it four of the nine brightest stars in the sky, and it is visible to everyone in the world during the last and first months of the year. This prominence has given these stars a place in all cultures: fire sticks to the Aztecs, a white tiger to the Chinese, an armed king to the early Irish, a big bird to the Polynesians, and a tortoise to the Mayans. Orion even appears as Smati-Osiris, the Barley God, in the *Egyptian Book of the Dead* from nearly 4,000 years ago. Resting on the equator, however, the constellation lacks the steadfastness of the North Star, rising and setting, moving constantly through the sky, shifting with and the seasons.

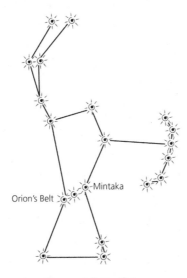

The constellation Orion.

Orion's right shoulder is the red giant Betelgeuse, from the Arabic expression for "giant's shoulder" and often pronounced "Beetlejuice." It is one of the brightest stars in the sky. His lower half contains Rigel, a blue-white star that burns 37,000 times more brilliantly than our sun. His sword contains one of a small number of nebulae visible to the naked eye—these swirling masses of hot gases act as breeding grounds for new stars—and his sword hangs from a belt. It is Orion's belt that is used to find direction.

The belt consists of an asterism of three bright stars. It is easy to identify because it is the only place in the night sky where three such brilliant stars form a straight line. The belt as a whole rises in the east and sets in the west. Mintaka is the northwestern-most of the stars in the belt. The northern aspect is important because the belt as a whole sits just south of the equator, so the northern-most star is the one closest to the equator. Its western aspect is relevant because it means that it is the one that rises first of the three. This means that the leading star in Orion's belt will rise within 1 degree of east and set within 1 degree of west.

In low latitudes the night sky is a mix of northern and southern stars. Here is an example of a southern star and the North Star being used together as a means of natural navigation. Canopus is the second brightest star in the sky after Sirius. It is a southern star, sitting close to 53 degrees south of the celestial equator. It will always rise well south of east and set well south of west. A Bedouin poet combined his observation of this star and his knowledge of the North Star, known to him as al-Jidi, in composing the following lines to describe a camel rider heading southeast:

Ahutt al-Jidi 'ald wirk il-matiyyah

W'adhri naharhd 'an Suhayl al-yimain

(I put Polaris on the thigh of my mount
While shielding her throat from Canopus south)

The Celestial Sphere and the Sun

As we have seen, the celestial sphere rotates about the earth at a constant speed, completing one revolution every twenty-three hours and fifty-six minutes. Returning to a true physical understanding of the universe for a moment, it is understood that this is the time it takes for the Earth to complete one revolution on its axis. So why do we think of a day as lasting twenty-four hours? In the time that the Earth has taken to revolve on its axis, it has also moved 1/365th of the way around the sun in its orbit, too. This means that it has to rotate a little bit farther before the sun appears back where it started—an extra four minutes to be precise, and hence the twenty-four-hour day.

The timing of our day is dictated by our relationship with the sun rather than the stars—we have a solar day, not a sidereal one. What this means is that the celestial sphere is rotating slightly faster than the sun. In other words, the stars appear to rise four minutes earlier each day, but then 365 lots of four minutes makes twenty-four hours. So each year the stars come back to the starting point, and the race that the sun always loses can begin again.

The North Star does not move, and although the circumpolar stars appear in different places at different times of the year, they never set. All the other stars appear above and below the horizon at both different times of the night and year. So, for example, Orion is known as a winter constellation in the northern hemisphere and the Navigator's Triangle, a group of stars made up of Deneb, Altair, and Vega, is also nicknamed the Summer Triangle. The relationship between the stars that are visible and the time of year reveals another celestial calendar, as do the rising and setting positions of the sun.

The "heliacal rising" of a star is the expression used to explain the day when a star becomes visible just before sunrise. The heliacal rising of the brightest star in the sky, Sirius, had seasonal implications for most ancient peoples. Pliny the Elder referred to it when explaining the time of year at which voyages to India were undertaken. It was known as Sothis to the ancient Egyptians and used to predict the rising of the Nile from as early as 4241 BC. More recently, its appearance in the evening sky in spring has been used as the cue for men in the Kalahari Desert to begin their second phase of school. The rising and setting rhythms of the Pleiades were used to trigger the harvesting and sowing of grain in the Mediterranean, and Arcturus's rising signaled the start of the geese-hunting season for the Australian Aboriginals. The seasonal habits of the stars were even linked to the lustfulness of women and feebleness of men at certain times of the year by the Greek poet Hesiod.

The timings of the appearance of the stars may change, but their position on the sphere and hence their rising and setting positions do not—at least not during the course of a lifetime. There is in fact a very gradual change taking place, brought about by a process called the "precession of the equinoxes."

Although the Earth spins regularly on its axis, around 130 BC Hipparchus noticed (and was probably the first to do so) that its rotation was not completely steady. If the Earth is imagined spinning like a child's top, then one might perceive a slow wobble in that perpetual motion. The North Pole, as seen from above, moves very slowly in a circle. It takes 25,800 years to complete this circle, and so the changes it causes in our view of the celestial sphere cannot be detected in a lifetime. The only reason this incredibly slow change has any relevance is that natural navigators spend a fair amount of time looking a long way back, to how journeys were undertaken thousands of years ago.

Since the axis of rotation is moving very slowly, the north celestial pole moves in a circle around the sphere, too. This means that Polaris has not always been so close to the celestial pole. In 10,000 years the North Star will be Deneb, and after another 4,000 it will be Vega. Looking back to ancient Egyptian and Greek times, Polaris was not as good an indicator of true north as it is now and will be for the next few hundred years. For the Egyptians of 3,000 BC the star Thuban, in the constellation Draco, was closest to the celestial pole, so this is the star which would have been used for alignment of the pyramids.

The precession of the equinoxes is not a pressing issue—it does not change the night sky over the course of several lifetimes—so having accepted that the ancients may refer to the stars with some subtle differences to the modern view, it is safe to ignore this principle for the rest of our navigating lives.

The Planets

The planets can bring fascination, joy, and intrigue in equal help-ings, but are much less useful to the natural navigator than the stars. However, a basic knowledge of the planets is important for anyone using the night sky to navigate—not least to avoid mistak-enly identifying them as stars. The planets neither move in the exact same way as the stars nor are they exactly similar in appear-ance, and yet they are regularly confused with the stars.

The easiest way to distinguish a planet from a star is by appear-ance. The planets are in our solar system and are therefore a lot closer to us than any stars other than the sun. This makes them visible as small discs or crescents when viewed through a tele-scope. Seen with the naked eye they can appear like stars in brightness, color, and shape, but the light we see is subtly differ-ent. Starlight is from a smaller pinpoint source, and as that "point" of light hits the Earth's atmosphere it gets bounced around, causing the stars to twinkle or "scintillate." Light from the planets is from a slightly broader apparent source, and so even though it gets bounced around, it also averages out giving a more constant or steady light. Put simply, planets do not twinkle in the way that stars do.

The Greek word *planetai* means wanderers, and that is a fair description of the motion of the planets. We know now that the planets are all held in orbit around the sun by gravity and there-fore circle it with dependable regularity. However, the Earth is also orbiting around the sun, and so our view of the other planets is complicated by something called retrograde motion. This is an observational problem caused by the fact that planets that sit beyond the Earth in the solar system orbit the sun more slowly than Earth. In other words, their year lasts longer than ours. This makes them appear to move slowly one way in the sky, until the Earth "overtakes" them on the inside and then they appear to briefly move in the opposite direction. This is something that caused great confusion for mankind before Copernicus.

The position that each planet will appear in our sky at any given time cannot be deduced by purely natural means. Although perfectly logical, the apparent motion of a particular planet is complex enough to require tables or software to be able to predict. There are however some basic principles that are worth knowing.

While the motion of a planet over time is not easy to predict, their movement in the sky over a few days is negligible, so once identified, their position relative to the stars around them will not change over the course of an evening or even over the course of several nights. The other important thing to understand is that

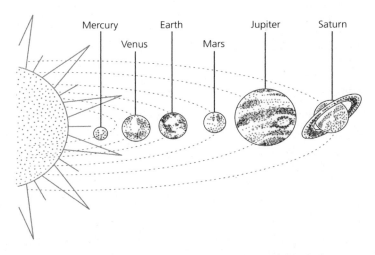

The planets in our solar system that are easily visible with the naked eye.

the planets move in two distinct ways. The Earth's daily rotation causes all celestial objects, planets included, to appear to rise over the eastern horizon and set on the western. If viewed from northern latitudes, then, like all celestial objects, their highest point in the sky will be due south. This arcing motion, from east to west, is the dominant one in the night sky, but it is not the same as the planets' motion due to their own orbit around the sun, which in turn is determined by how close they are to the sun.

All the planets orbit the sun within a similar broad band or plane. This means that they all appear in a band of the night sky within 30 degrees of the celestial equator. However, only five planets are easily visible to the naked eye. These are Mercury, Venus, Mars, Jupiter, and Saturn.

Mercury, the closest planet to the sun, races around it such that a Mercury year lasts only eighty-eight days. This proximity to the sun makes it difficult to see in the sky, because it is usually blotted out by the sun itself. It will never be more than 28 degrees or three extended fist-widths from the sun, and can only be seen at dawn or dusk. It also means that its position changes relatively rapidly, a fact not lost on the Polynesians, who called it Na-holo-holo, "running to and fro." If you see a bright white object on the horizon just before dawn or after dusk and you have eliminated the bright stars and other planets, you may have caught a glimpse of Mercury, which is something that not many can claim to have done, including, ironically, Copernicus himself.

The next in line, the brilliant white Venus, is slightly farther from the sun and therefore a lot easier to see. It is never more than 47 degrees from the sun, just under five extended fist-widths, but this extra distance makes it a much more significant feature of the early morning and evening skies. It is the brightest object in the sky after the sun and moon.

The ancients never ignored it, but due to its appearance at either end of the day they were divided in their opinion, some seeing two separate objects and others a roaming planet. Venus was the Roman goddess of love and beauty, but the Greeks knew it as Phosphorus in the morning and Hesperus in the evening. In Africa it has been known variously as the "moon's wife," "evening fugitive," and the wonderful "peeper into pots," as it appeared close to mealtimes at either end of the day.

Venus spends about eight months of the year as a low bright early evening object on the horizon, before its orbit takes it in front of the sun and it becomes invisible for eight days. It then reemerges in the early morning and can be found close to dawn for another eight months before it disappears behind the sun for fifty days and then the cycle begins again.

Venus can be a good ally for journeys once you have identified it. If Venus is a bright signpost in the southwestern sky one night, it will be there the next. The best way to use it is not normally as the primary way of finding direction, but as an excellent way of holding your course.

I remember exploring the South Downs in West Sussex one winter's evening in 2009. After the sun set most other walkers headed home. I stayed back and kept walking to keep the cold out as the two-day-old crescent moon, Venus and then Jupiter and even Mercury became briefly visible in the southwest. All of them set except for Venus, which stayed well above the horizon and gave me the confidence to cut through some dark woods. Finding direction from the stars is great, but the beacon-friendliness of Venus on a night like that, announcing itself through even the tangled black yew branches, was joyous. It helped me not to lose faith in my impulsive foray, and I emerged, one or two scratches later, from the woods with its white torch still declaring southwest.

Mars is the red planet. Named for the Roman god of war, it was associated with death for the Babylonians. More recently it has come to hold a particular fascination due to its theoretical ability to sustain life. We may now be searching for evidence of microorganisms and not little green men, but the discovery of any form of life on another planet would shake our view of the universe as vigorously as did the Copernican revolution.

I have a soft spot for Mars, as it kept me company as I sailed alone across the Atlantic in December 2007. It is not very useful in finding direction, but can throw off your reading of the night sky if you fail to recognize it. If you see a prominent red star close to the celestial equator when you are not expecting to see one, you should consider the possibility of its being Mars.

A modern twist to the Mars story is the fact that spacecraft finding their way to Mars rely on astro-navigation, electronically gauging the positions of the stars to help them find their way. In this age, where the least technical person can use GPS technology to find their way around on Earth, the pioneering journeys in our solar system are still use methods that Cook would have understood—even if he would have raised an eyebrow at the computers that do the work.

Jupiter is the largest planet in our solar system and an excellent reflector of light, making it easy to spot. As it is another bright white planet, it is regularly mistaken for Venus. However, it sits far enough out in the solar system that its orbit around the sun takes considerably longer. Once found, it does not go anywhere in a hurry, taking a year to move through a constellation and twelve to complete the cycle.

Like most of the visible planets, Jupiter can be used to hold a course even if it is not used to find one. One of Scott's polar companions, Apsley Cherry-Garrard, found some fondness for it in this context, even in what became known as "The Worst Journey in the World": "Generally we steered by Jupiter, and I never see him now without recalling his friendship in those days."

The yellowish Saturn is farther out still and remains within one constellation for several years. It is best known for its rings, but these can only be seen through a telescope. Its axis of rotation is tilted in the same way as that of Earth, and so it experiences seasons, each one lasting seven years. Although rarely of use in natural navigation, it is possible that Saturn features in one of the most famous pathfinding stories of all time. In 6 BC, Jupiter, Mars, and Saturn would all have been visible low on the horizon, an unusual and striking sight. Could they have been the inspiration or guide for the three wise men?

Astrology

Since earliest times, people have looked to nature as a guide, both physical and spiritual. Astrology is but one of many methods of attempting to divine the future from observing nature, but to anyone interested in the night sky, and the modern and ancient use of it, astrological conventions are inescapable. There remains a clear link between astronomy and astrology and whether or not you believe in astrology, there is plenty of accurate astronomical information to be found in astrological sources. Johannes Kepler ranks as one of the greatest ever astronomers; he also cast horoscopes to help pay the bills. For all the opinions on either side about astrology, no one can deny that it is a powerful idea. This is demonstrated by the suspicion with which it was held by Church and State alike throughout the ages. Plato's uncle, Critias, was convinced that strange goings-on in the heavens, like eclipses, were the work of cunning statesmen as a device to keep the peace with the populace.

The Christian Church has always rejected astrology, since it goes against the notion of free will. This is probably why it was the Church, in the form of Bishop Isidore of Seville, that formally divided astronomy from astrology in the seventh century.

Colorful figures like the sixteenth-century astrologer Arcandam, who held that a man born under the constellation of Sagittarius would be "thrice wedded, and very fond of vegetables," have probably not helped defend astrology from its critics. Whatever your thoughts on the accuracy or otherwise of astrological predictions, the irrefutable truth is that our lives are strongly influenced by celestial objects: our daily and annual patterns by the sun, any sea journeys by the moon. So the real question is where we think this influence stops, not whether or not it exists.

Shooting Stars and Strange Glows

The Earth's atmosphere is hit by approximately one million particles per hour that burn brightly and then turn to dust that settles over the planet continuously. These are meteors or shooting stars. Very occasionally, a lump from an asteroid will make it through the atmosphere all the way to the ground and qualify as a meteorite. The largest one ever found was discovered in Namibia in 1920. The Hoba meteorite is nearly ten feet across and is believed to weigh sixty tons.

Meteors have a relationship with time and direction. You are likely to see more shooting stars after midnight than before, because this is when your part of Earth is facing "forward" as it moves in its orbit around the sun. Think of how many more raindrops hit the front windscreen of your car than the rear window. At certain times of the year the Earth's orbit will take it through the dust trail of a comet. In October, the Earth passes through the trail of Halley's comet and so we experience the Orionid meteor showers, an increase in the number of shooting stars that appear to originate close to the constellation Orion.

Dust in the solar system can cause another light phenomenon known as the zodiacal light. A band of dust stretches out in our solar system in the same plane as the planets, and when the sun reflects off this near dawn and dusk we can sometimes see it as a glow over the eastern or western horizons. The glow usually takes the form of a rounded triangle, with a broader base near the horizon.

Comets are very different from meteors. Some, like Halley's, are well understood, since we have known about them for hundreds of years. Comets are not used to find direction, but can be used like the planets to hold a course. Although it is popularly known that comets have tails, what is not so well known is that the tail will always stretch away from the sun, even if the comet is itself moving away from the sun. This is because the comet is not moving through an atmosphere and leaving a trail in the way a steam train might. Instead, its tail is being caused by a constant wind of particles from the sun itself. These same charged particles that push the comet's tail away from the sun also hit the Earth's atmosphere and leave their mark. The northern and southern lights, or aurora borealis and aurora australis, are seen as impressive arcs, bands, and lines of green light with hints of other colors. They are most clearly visible at high latitudes, because those charged particles from the sun are channeled in that way by the Earth's own magnetic field.

Apsley Cherry-Garrard witnessed some impressive displays in the Antarctic:

> The aurora was always before us as we traveled east, more beautiful than any seen by previous expeditions wintering in McMurdo Sound, where Erebus must have hidden the most brilliant displays. Now most of the sky was covered with swinging, swaying curtains which met in a great whirl overhead: lemon yellow, green and orange.

It is not surprising that the aurorae have featured strongly in the culture of the Eskimo people, living as they do in extreme latitudes, and there is good evidence that the lights have been used for navigating. The lights have a strong east–west bias—American anthropologist Richard Nelson, who spent time conducting anthropological research in the Arctic in the 1960s, found this alignment existed in almost all of the sightings he made.

The Milky Way

In Jiangja in Jiangsu Province, China, there are 4,000-year-old cliff carvings that contain depictions of the sun, moon, and some stars. The Milky Way can also be found on the cliff, easily recognizable by its signature light and dark patches. The carver could not have known that each of the light patches in the Milky Way represented millions of stars and clouds of gas. This is our galaxy, our home in the broadest sense.

The light milky and dark patches that give our galaxy its own unique fingerprint in the sky can be used as a celestial map to help us find other objects. A famous dark area called the Coal Sack can be found next to the Southern Cross and can be used to identify that important constellation.

If the navigational goal is of a more ambitious sort, then the way to reach the center of our galaxy is to aim for the southern hemisphere constellation Sagittarius, which can be found in the clouds of the Milky Way and looks a little bit like a teapot.

Time and Space

The relationship between time, navigation, and the stars is a cozy one. Since the celestial sphere moves at a uniform speed around the Earth, it is possible to tell the time by looking at the stars. However, it is a bit like learning to tell the time all over again, for three reasons. First, the northern stars rotate counterclockwise, so in the northern hemisphere the clock has to be read in the opposite direction to a conventional clock. Second, the clock is a twenty-four-hour one, which takes a bit of getting used to. And third, because the celestial sphere and the sun do not move at exactly the same speed there is some adjusting to be done to the time that is read off the sky clock. If this fails to deter you, then a concise, but still demanding, explanation of how to try it can be found in the Notes section at the end of the book.

When the locals from Baffin Island, in the Canadian Arctic, found themselves a long way out to sea, on drift ice, at night and out of sight of land, they would hold their left hand out and align it with Tukturjuit, the Caribou (the Big Dipper), to point the way to land.

The stars have appeared as dependable friends for travelers all over the globe for thousands of years, often when other guides have failed them. Whether they help to find the way or just add some texture to a journey, they can only enrich our experience and so it is a tragedy that so few feel able to engage with the stars.

Using the sky as a tool for natural navigation doesn't preclude looking above us with wonder. It is possible to learn how to find north in under a minute, but that does not prevent study of all the visible constellations. It does not prevent developing an interest in the nebulae and supernovae. It does not stop anyone from looking at the Andromeda Galaxy, two million light-years away and the most distant object visible to the naked eye, and sharing that experience with the Islamic astronomer al-Sufi, who wrote about it a thousand years ago.

We shall leave the subject of the night sky, for now, with some practical advice. Do not let the ease with which you find direction allow complacency to creep in. The celestial sphere continues to turn after the sun has risen, but even the brightest of stars is quickly shrouded from view by the light of day.

If you are settling in for the evening and find the direction you need clearly from the stars, then plant a stick in the ground and line it up with another stick, rock, or landmark so that you can set off in the right direction the following morning. It is something you might be grateful for after the daylight or clouds have blotted out all trace of the stars. If you get carried away you may manage to build something substantial, something that will have archaeologists scratching their heads and rubbing their chins 2,000 years from now.

CHAPTER 4
The Fickle Moon

I can sit and gaze and gaze, my eyes entranced by the
dream-glow yonder in the west, where the moon's
thin, pale, silver sickle is dipping its point into the
blood; and my soul is borne beyond the glow, to the
sun, so far off now—and to the homecoming!

—Fridtjof Nansen

Among the Xhosa of South Africa it is held that the sea is filled
with moons, ready to replace the old, spent ones. The moon's
crescent is seen as a cause for hope in some cultures, but as a
basin pouring illness out into the world in others. It is among the
most elusive and yet most fascinating of signs for the navigator. It
is foolish to ignore it and yet impossible to master it.

"It" does not seem the right pronoun—"she" feels better.
There have always been feminine associations with the moon.
There are physical, spiritual, and etymological connections
between the moon and menstruation. The moon's cycle and
phases have represented pregnancy, birth, and rebirth, and in
some parts of the world, like Austria, girls with small breasts were
encouraged to expose them to full moonlight.

The moon has also been connected with the life and growth of plants, in both ancient cultures and more recently, when there has been a renewal of interest in the principles of "biodynamics." This involves keeping the agrarian cycle in tune with celestial phases, particularly the moon, the idea being that in the same way that the world's oceans are affected by the moon's gravitational pull, so, too, are the sap and roots of plants. This is old thinking, not new. Pliny the Elder wrote that the best time to cut down trees was when "the moon is in conjunction with the sun, that day being called the interlinium, or sometimes the 'moon's silence.'" He also reported that Tiberius Caesar used this theory to time the felling of the larches needed to rebuild the bridge at Naumachia.

There is both simplicity and complexity to be found in all things astronomical. The moon is no exception. Natural navigators need to be concerned mostly with light, time, tide and direction. Of these, light is the most familiar to us all. Apsley Cherry-Garrard was saved by the moon's light in Antarctica:

> There had been no light all day, clouds obscured the moon, we had not seen her since yesterday. And quite suddenly a little patch of clear sky drifted, as it were, over her face, and she showed us three paces ahead a great crevasse with just a shining icy lid not much thicker than glass.

Apsley Cherry-Garrard was saved from a "very sticky death," but we have all experienced the joys of a moonlit world, bright and yet strangely foreign, stark, and harsh in places.

Each culture has interpreted the patterns on the face of the moon differently, partly because the orientation of the moon changes depending on the observer's latitude. Wherever you are in the world, the waxing and waning of the moon remains constant—a full moon is full the world over—but the moon's orientation varies as you travel north or south, so in some places its features will appear as though upside down.

In most cultures, travel by day has always been favored over travel by night. In some, such as the Gwi of the Kalahari Desert, stars are never used to navigate, so a nighttime journey will only be undertaken if there is sufficient moonlight to make the daytime methods of landmark recognition possible. An understanding of how much light can be expected is part of the preparation for a night expedition, not least because a bright moon will illuminate the land, but will also blot out a lot of the stars in its part of the sky. Marvin Creamer, who, as I've mentioned, circumnavigated the world without navigational instruments, looked forward to some help from the moon as he closed on the shores of New Zealand during his trip around the world.

Those who ply their trade by night—fishermen, for example—know both the importance of the amount of moonlight and the differences in the appearance of land or sea in moonlight. If you need to be able to read the sea's surface in detail (if you are searching for a buoy, for instance), it is easiest to do in sunlight if the sun is on your back. But at night, if the moon is up and the sky is cloudless, then you get the best visibility of the surface by looking into the moon. This can be critical in a man-overboard situation.

The Gwi of the Kalahari Desert throw animal bones at the first sight of the crescent moon in the evening and implore that it will help them to not wander and get lost. The aims of this chapter are not far removed from this simple goal.

Whenever we see the moon, night or day, we are witnessing a moment in the relationship between the Earth, moon, and sun. This relationship is defined by time, or it may be more accurate to say that the relationship defines time.

Time and date conventions have endured centuries of artificial manipulation until their roots in celestial observations are no longer widely understood. Struggle as they may, clocks and watches consistently fail to mark true midday. They are nearly always wrong in celestial terms. And these conventions become even more convoluted when we consider calendars.

The modern Western calendar is shaped by the Earth–sun relationship; it defines the year, but the moon has its own influence. The reasons for the sun's dominance are essentially practical: We can plan according to seasons that are meaningful. But there are also spiritual associations with the celestial influence on time and date, and these are often focused around the moon. Both the Jewish and Islamic calendars are lunar and, like all things religious, practicality fails to dominate. A lunar month is 29.5 days long and so twelve lunar months add up to 354 days, falling short of a solar year by eleven days. Islamic holy days are consistent with the moon, but fall earlier each year with regard to a solar calendar—the lunar calendar runs fast relative to a solar one by ten days.

The Christian Church is far from immune to the moon's rhythms. The date of Easter is determined in relation to lunar phases, and there was a heated debate between the eastern and western branches of the Church over how to calculate its date until the Council of Nicea in 325 AD settled matters. Easter now falls on the first Sunday following the first full moon after the spring equinox.

Once all the political, religious, and cultural influences and sensitivities have been taken into consideration, it becomes clear that there are a number of conventions for describing the passage of time, all of which have their roots in the same celestial objects and all of which are for the most part incompatible. What a very human mess. For this reason, getting back to our common experience, stripping things right back to easily perceived celestial phenomena, could be a powerful way of ridding ourselves of these artificial differences. If you arrange to meet a stranger, perhaps from an isolated tribe, at a certain latitude and longitude on June 7 at 6 PM, you may find yourself all alone. If, however, you arrange to meet anyone in the world under a certain dominant tree as the sun sets and the full moon rises, you are far more likely to see them again. The anthropologist George Silberbauer found he could use moon phases as a calendar that could be easily understood and communicated during his time in the Kalahari Desert.

The lunar cycle can still be regarded as the universal language of date and time; the one that all humanity understood before we created artificial structures that confused matters. The full moons have been used as natural markers in the calendar by those closest to the land for millennia. The legacy of this can be seen in expressions like "Harvest Moon," which is the full moon nearest the autumn equinox. For the tribes of the northeastern United States, this moon was followed by the Hunter's Moon, when the deer are ripe and ready. There are all sorts of other weird and wonderful examples: In Madagascar there is the "Bulls Seek Shade Moon" and the "Guinea Fowl Sleeps Moon." The Siberian

Ostiak have a "Ducks and Geese Go Away Moon" and the Inuit mark time with "Sun is Possible," "Sun Gets Higher" and "Premature Seal Pups" moons.

A carved eagle bone found in a cave in France may contain the first evidence of man's interest in lunar phases. It dates back 32,000 years and has etched into it a series of curved marks that seem to correspond to each day of the moon's phases over a period of a month. Further north, in northeastern Scotland at a place called Castle Frazer, there are rings of standing stones that date from around 2000 BC. Archaeological work has shown that the alignment of these stones is consistent with a thorough understanding of the moon's cycle.

The moon orbits the Earth roughly in a plane from west to east and completes this orbit in a little over twenty-seven days. To make sense of how this appears from Earth, it is necessary to understand it in the context of the two other critical motions: the Earth's spin and its orbit around the sun. It might help to freeze the Earth's spin for a moment and ignore the sun. Now it is possible to imagine how the moon's orbit would appear from Earth. The moon would rise somewhere over the western horizon and move very slowly eastward until it set over the eastern horizon about two weeks later, two weeks after that it would rise again over the western horizon, and the cycle would repeat. This is quite counterintuitive, since we are used to everything rising in the east and setting in the west, but remember that this is what would be seen if the Earth was not spinning.

Now it is time to let the Earth spin again. The Earth spins at 15 degrees per hour counterclockwise when viewed from vertically above the North Pole. This makes anything in the sky appear to move from east to west at 15 degrees per hour—even if they are not actually moving. This is much faster than the apparent motion of the moon itself orbiting the Earth and so this becomes by far the dominant apparent motion. The moon appears to move from east to west, even though it is actually orbiting in the opposite direction. When we put these two motions together the result is that the moon rises in the east and sets in the west, but it is also moving slowly eastward relative to everything else in the sky, about its own width or half a degree per hour. It is still moving eastward relative to the stars and sun at the same speed that it would do if the Earth was still, but now the apparent motion from the Earth's spin is so great that it appears to be moving the other way, along with the sun and stars.

It is time to reintroduce the sun. The two key factors when considering the sun in relation to the moon are first that the brightness of the moon is a reflection of the sun's light—i.e., the moon emits no light of its own. Second, there are 29.5 days between successive full moons, not twenty-seven as there would be if the Earth and moon were not orbiting the sun. This is because the Earth and moon have moved relative to the sun since the start of the moon's orbital cycle.

What We See

The sun and moon appear to move in a similar plane from east to west, but because the moon's orbit makes it move slowly east in the sky, the sun appears to move marginally faster than the moon. If they are in the same place in the sky one day, then the following day the moon will have "slipped back" by 1/29.5th of the way, or approximately 12.2 degrees (one extended fist-width plus an extra knuckle). The following day it will have slipped another 12.2 degrees. After fifteen days the moon will be lagging the sun by 15 × 12.2 degrees, which is very nearly 180 degrees. Two weeks after that the moon will have slipped so far back that the sun will have caught up with it and the cycle begins again.

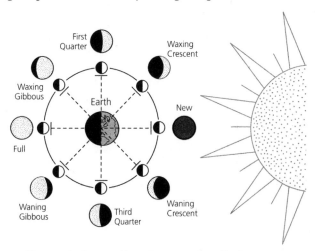

The moon's phases and how they appear from Earth.

Since the moon is only visible when it is reflecting the light of the sun, its position relative to the sun will determine how visible it is and the shape we see. When the sun and moon are in the same part of the sky, the moon will not be visible at all. This is the new moon. Two days after a new moon, the moon has slipped back just far enough that it might be possible to catch one edge of the moon reflecting sunlight toward us. This thin crescent will be about 25 degrees behind, i.e., east of the sun in the sky (two-and-a-half extended fist-widths). One week after a new moon, the moon is one quarter of the way through its "lagging" cycle, and this is called a first quarter moon. This causes some confusion, because we actually see half of the moon, the western half nearest the sun—the "quarter" in this case refers to the cycle, not the amount of the moon we can see. Fifteen days after a new moon, when the moon has slipped back 180 degrees, it is now opposite the sun, and being opposite the sun it acts as a full mirror. At this point we see the whole face of the moon as bright. This is the full moon. One week after a full moon, the moon is three-quarters of the way through its cycle, and again we only see one half of it, the eastern half nearest the sun. One week later the cycle has come full circle, back to the new moon. The key is to remember that the shape of the moon we see is influenced by how far the moon is around from the sun in its cycle. From nothing at new moon, to a sliver, to half, on to full and then reducing until it is back to nothing and a new moon again. Since the moon lags the sun by a fraction more each day, it follows that it must rise marginally later each day. On average the moon rises about fifty minutes later each day, which is the amount that tide times lag the previous day on average.

Getting Practical

Understanding the orbit of the moon and its phases is critical, but this does not on its own help with finding direction. To do that it is necessary to bring the moon down to Earth.

The moon appears to follow a similar path to the sun and other celestial objects. It rises in the east and sets in the west, and at one moment it is neither east nor west, when it reaches its highest point in the sky. Harking back to what we know about the sun, it is logical that the moon appears at its highest point in the sky at the moment it crosses the meridian of the observer, that is the north–south line that runs from the North Pole between the feet of the observer to the South Pole. In other words the moon must be due south or north when it is highest in the sky.

A bright moon will cast a good shadow, and a shadow stick can be used in exactly the same way as it is with the sun. The moon only needs to be bright enough to cast a shadow, it does not need to be a full moon, although of course this is when it is easiest. It is the motion of the moon that is important for this to work, not how much of it can be seen or its phase.

The shortest shadow cast by the moon will be a perfect north–south line. If you are well into the northern hemisphere, the shadow tip will point north and the base south. Nearer the equator, working out the orientation of the shadow becomes a lot more complex, and it is better to rely on other methods.

The next step is a deductive one. If the sun and moon both appear to move in an east–west plane, then it follows that when it is not a new moon and the sun and moon are not together, the moon must be roughly east or west of the sun. This means that the light side will point to the sun, which will appear roughly east or west of the moon. The bright side of the moon is acting as an approximate compass, pointing west or east. However, reading a compass in the sky is not very practical, so the best thing to do is to extend a tangent to the crescent line that separates light from dark down to the horizon. This line will be perpendicular to the direction of the sun and any line perpendicular to an east–west line is a north–south line; this line will touch the horizon reasonably close to south if viewed from a northern latitude. This method tends to work best when the moon is high in the sky.

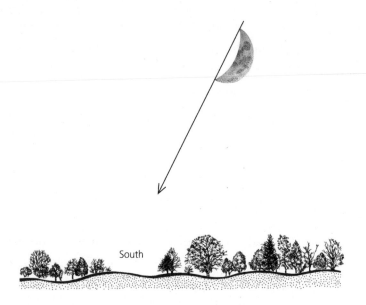

South

Using the crescent moon in the northern hemisphere.

The shadow stick method is very accurate, but can be impractical. The tangent method above is very practical but not nearly as accurate. What follows is the phase method, a beautiful method, because it encapsulates all the basic knowledge about the moon a navigator ever needs: its orbit, time, light, and phases. It is, however, difficult to grasp, and takes patience and practice.

To be able to find direction just by looking at the moon using the phase method requires three things: Some idea of what time it is, the more accurate then obviously the better; an ability to recognize roughly which stage the moon is at, i.e., the difference between a six-day-old and a four-day-old moon; some basic mental arithmetic.

It is a good idea to start with the most straightforward example of this method. During a new moon the moon cannot be seen since it is hidden in the sun's bright glare, but if it could, then it would be positioned in the same direction as the sun. That means that at midday the new moon must be due south from northern latitudes. At 6 AM the new moon will be close to east, and at 6 PM it will be close to west since it is moving across the sky in tandem with the sun. So far, so simple.

A full moon is opposite the sun, which means that at midday the sun is due south and the moon is opposite it, due north. It is invisible at midday, because it is "underground," but there are lots of times when it can be seen. At midnight, the roles are reversed, the sun is due north and invisible and the moon is now visible and approximately due south. At sunrise the full moon will be close to setting and therefore close to west, and at sunset the moon will be opposite again, it will be rising and close to east.

One week after the new moon is a first quarter moon. We see half of the moon's face, since it is quarter of the way round its complete cycle, but halfway from new to full. A first quarter moon is lagging the sun by quarter of a complete cycle or 90 degrees. If the sun is west, or 270 degrees, then the moon will be roughly 90 degrees behind that or 180 degrees, which is due south (from northern latitudes). In other words a first quarter moon will be due south at about 6 PM.

A third quarter moon is three-quarters of the way back round from a new moon. It is lagging the sun by 270 degrees, which is the same as saying that it is so far behind that it is actually 90 degrees ahead of the sun. When the sun rises it will be close to east or 90 degrees and a third quarter moon will be 90 degrees ahead of that, at 180 degrees or due south. A third quarter moon is due south at about 6 AM.

Things get more complicated when we look beyond those (relatively) straightforward examples. Let's try something a little more complex. Let's imagine that you are looking at this moon at 9 PM:

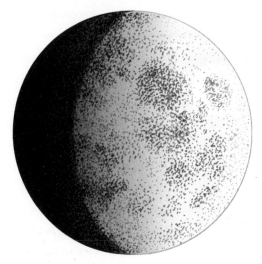

Gazing up at the sky, it is possible to make the following deductions. The moon appears to be older than first quarter, but younger than a full moon. It appears to be halfway between the two, so a best guess is that it is a ten-day-old moon. This means that it will lag the sun by about 10 × 12 degrees or 120 degrees. At 9 PM the sun will be roughly halfway between its 6 PM direction and its midnight direction, which is roughly halfway between west and north. Northwest is 315 degrees, so the moon is likely to be roughly 315 degrees minus 120 degrees, which is 195 degrees or close to south.

If this method seems fussy and unwieldy, it will become far less so with honing, but one of its real attractions is its rarity. There are not many people in the world familiar with its use. It sits between scientific knowledge and natural experience, between an ancient understanding and a modern view of the world. As such it is unique.

The Moon, Tide, and Direction

The extremes of tidal height and speeds are called "spring tides," and they occur shortly after the sun's and the moon's gravitational influences are aligned. This happens when the moon and sun are either in line, a new moon, or opposite, a full moon. Neap tides, the narrowest range, when heights at high and low water are as close to each other as they get, occur between the lunar extremes, shortly after we see half of the moon.

It is possible to refine this knowledge further and bring lunar direction into the mix. This is possible because lunar phase, time, tides, and lunar direction are all interrelated. The height of tidal water and even its direction of flow are determined by the Earth, moon, sun, and time. With a lot of practice and perhaps some local knowledge, it occasionally becomes possible to look at a waterline and the direction of the water's flow and know what direction the moon will be. This is at the far reaches of natural navigation.

It does not have to stop there, though. There is a lot of fun to be had by trying to understand the fuller picture and making new connections. Here is one example. Fishing is usually best when there is a large tidal range, because the faster currents carry prey, and the predators like to maneuver themselves into position to make the most of this fast conveyor belt of food. Experienced fishermen know this and will position themselves to catch the predators. Voilà! The direction of the moon can be guessed from the number of fishing rods that can be counted at a particular time of day.

CHAPTER 5

The Sea

The journeys and ideas that dominate our perception of exploration and navigating across oceans mostly come from an instrument age, long after the first journeys of exploration were made. It is worth recalling that Western explorers did not in general achieve fame for their discoveries of uninhabited lands. They may have added places to maps and increased knowledge of foreign lands, but they mostly went where others had gone long before.

This is an aspect of exploration that receives scant attention, because there are so few facts available—we know very little about the thousands of voyages that populated lands all over the globe. Some of these original explorers will have walked across now sunken land bridges, unaware that they were crossing over to a new landmass, or have been hostages to fortune, blown off course until perishing or beaching on a new atoll. However, there must also have been many deliberate voyages of exploration.

The Norwegian ethnologist and adventurer Thor Heyerdahl was convinced that the Polynesian islands were populated by South American voyagers who had sailed there using the easterly wind and sea currents. He built a balsa wood raft that he named *Kon-Tiki* and set off from Peru with five companions in 1947, determined to prove his point. After a journey lasting 101 days, he landed on an island east of Tahiti. He proved beyond question the technical feasibility of such a voyage having been undertaken in ancient times. But despite his determination and the hardships he endured, it is now generally accepted that the genetic and anthropological evidence points to a migration of peoples from the Asian mainland.

While we are increasingly able to use scientific techniques to determine certain aspects of these journeys, such as the direction of migration, we still know close to nothing about the methods employed by these earliest explorers and navigators. We do know, of course, that they would have had to have been far more in touch with the navigational clues afforded by the natural world than we are today.

Today even small yacht leisure sailing is in the embrace of electronic navigation. It is quite easy now to achieve the status of Yachtmaster (which in the UK is certified by the Royal Yachting Association) and other qualifications without any real understanding of how water behaves, where to expect the moon and stars, or even where the sun rises and sets each day. What is more extraordinary is that this does not mean modern skippers are less capable or more at risk. But it does mean that many of them will undertake voyages across much duller and more two-dimensional seas than did our ancestors.

This chapter is about the many ways of understanding direction at sea that require no instruments, techniques that have been used by both ancient and modern seafarers. It is possible to enrich a sea voyage through a knowledge of these methods without throwing all the instruments overboard. They add an extra awareness of the natural world that can be enjoyed from the deck of a large vessel, in a small sailing dinghy, or even by the fireside.

Thirty thousand years ago our ancestors, the Cro-Magnons, had settled in Europe, developed sophisticated tools, and created artworks that included paintings and sculptures, and their brain capacity was actually larger than ours. Despite this, it is likely the first sea journeys would have been undertaken by accident or out of desperation and that the deliberate art of nautical navigation developed quite late relative to land travel. Life must have been hard enough without adding another layer of complexity and risk. We will probably never know exactly how man's relationship with sea travel began. (The first tangible evidence comes much later, beyond Europe, where images of ships began to appear on Egyptian artifacts from about 5,000 years ago. This is as far back as any real historical understanding of nautical navigation can be taken.)

The Mediterranean was a cradle for sophisticated civilization, but also for maritime development. It was ideal for this role as it had many physical attributes that made seafaring less forbidding than in other parts of the world, like northern Europe for example.

The Mediterranean climate guarantees many clear days and nights, making orientation by the sun and the stars more dependable. Its tides are negligible for the most part. Its coastlines are typically steeper and lack the rocks and long shelving shoals that are lethal to a voyager without intimate knowledge of a new coastline. I once spent two weeks navigating a yacht around the southwestern coast of Turkey without the use of any electronics and employing as few instruments as safely possible. It was an exercise that was made significantly more relaxing by the knowledge of the topography of the area that came from inspecting the charts. Unlike many coasts, the rocks in that part of Turkey descend underwater at a steep angle, so that it is possible in some places to be close enough to touch the rocks themselves and still be in a safe depth of water.

No discussion of early maritime navigation is complete without mention of "coast hugging." Anyone more used to land than sea, and this must have included the earliest navigators, has a tendency to want to remain near to the hard familiarity of land. However, anyone who has experience of the sea comes to know that being near the coast is much more risky and potentially perilous than having plenty of "sea room." Many more ships have been wrecked in a gale by being close to land than by exposure to open sea.

The very earliest navigators would almost certainly have been coast huggers. Who in their right mind would climb into an untested vessel and head as far away from the land as possible into the unknown? One can then imagine the next generation of navigators watching the first boats getting wrecked along the coast and realizing that a little distance is no bad thing. That is the process of all human development and knowledge building. Some brave souls make a leap of faith, and if they succeed they are heroes; if they fail, the next in line step over their bodies and try a different approach.

As the fertile ancient Mediterranean became home to burgeoning societies with growing wealth, this in turn led to a desire to trade, which probably led to the development of maritime techniques. In time, these Mediterranean societies became maritime ones.

These factors explain why the Mediterranean region offers up some of the earliest examples of methods of nautical navigation. These first examples come swaddled in art and myth and it is here, too, that we get a feel for the earliest experiences of the potential terror of the sea. Odysseus held on to a tree and narrowly escaped the spewing monster of Charybdis, an episode that was probably inspired by the real-life dangers of sailing too close to a whirlpool in the Strait of Messina.

The Mediterranean looms large in any accounts of this nascent art, but nautical developments were taking place in other parts of the world, where different challenges led to different solutions. In most of the world, ships passed each other, and there was trade, borrowed knowledge, and, inevitably, rivalry. (Ahmad ibn Fadlan, a tenth-century Arab writer, described the Vikings as "the filthiest people God ever made.") There were, however, some societies, like those in the Pacific, which developed in extreme geographical isolation, since less than one percent of the Pacific is land. For hundreds of years, the Pacific sat apart from the major trade routes and so the cross-fertilization of navigational ideas was limited. One result of this was that the unique navigation methods that were developed in the Pacific remain distinct and different to this day. Instruments arrived in the Pacific hundreds of years after most other areas, and so the natural awareness and skills that all seafaring cultures must once have shared were better preserved in the Pacific Islands than anywhere else. Captain James Cook was profoundly impressed by the Pacific Islanders' use of the sun, moon, and stars.

The Heavens

On December 21, 1982, Marvin Creamer headed into the Atlantic aboard his yacht, *Globe Star*. He had persuaded a crew to join him on his bid to sail around the world without the use of any nautical instruments. No compass, no sextant, no clock and, of course, no GPS. He returned safely eighteen months later, and later wrote of the voyage: "What we demonstrated is that information taken from the sea and sky can be used for fairly accurate and fairly safe navigation on a world-wide basis."

Unsurprisingly, perhaps, Creamer achieved his goal by using almost all of the known natural methods for shaping a course, determining position, and making landfall. He also added some pioneering ones of his own.

As Creamer neatly summarizes, there are two broad approaches to natural navigation at sea, just as there are on land. There are clues from the surface, in this case the wind and the sea itself, and those from the sky. The sky is the first place natural navigators should look. If the weather allows, then it is often possible to garner more accurate information from the sky, at day or night, than in any other way. At sea, the sun and the celestial sphere envelop the navigator and become of paramount importance.

The use of the sun at sea differs from its use on land in two ways. First, the use of shadows is not practical on small boats, since setting up a steady platform that does not rotate is almost impossible.

Second, there are not nearly as many indirect clues available to us. The water does not store useful information about the sun's path in the way the land does, and there are no plants that will yield clues. This means that the sun itself must always be used directly, particularly at sunrise and sunset.

To work out your direction at sea using the sun, it is very useful to know what direction the sun will be rising and setting for your latitude and time of year. If you do not have this information, it is possible, by following the methods discussed in the chapter about the sun, to make an estimate using an understanding of your latitude and the season. If you correctly employ this method, you are unlikely to be out by more than 10 degrees.

If you need to work out the direction of sunrise and sunset from your location from scratch, then you will have to estimate it using the stars. This means having your wits about you at twilight, the only time when the direction of the sun and stars can be discerned in a similar time frame. At dawn, the direction in which the sun rises can be estimated by comparing it to the stars visible near the horizon. This can then be used to predict the direction of the sun at the other end of the day. If the sun rises a few degrees south of Orion's belt in the morning, then it has risen a few degrees south of east and will set a few degrees south of west in the evening.

The other method for working out the direction of the sun without the use of shadows is with time. If you have access to a clock, you can work out when the sun is highest in the sky, i.e. crossing your meridian, and therefore due north or south by timing sunrise and sunset and calculating the midpoint between these. It is also possible to work backward from tables, but both a watch and tables are moving away from pure natural navigation.

Knowing the sun's bearing when it rises, the direction it moves through at local "real" midday, and where it sets provides us with three key points in the arc. The art of interpolation is needed to calculate all points of the arc within these three. Some Pacific Islanders are still able to steer using the sun by making these mental interpolations almost automatically. This is the result of thousands of hours spent at sea. The best way to emulate these seasoned sailors is to become familiar with the sun's arc and constantly test yourself against a compass or tables until your confidence grows. It is possible to become consistently more accurate over the course of a single week. It helps to understand the science, but this is definitely an art and like most arts, demands much practice.

The stars have been used by maritime navigators for as long as boats existed, but the strongest traditions are again found in the Pacific. Several important factors helped to create the perfect breeding ground for these skills. The sea was omnipresent and a primary source of food and therefore culturally viewed in a positive way. There are parts of the world, some of the Indonesian islands for example, where mountains are revered and seas feared, but the Polynesians and Micronesians must have worked out early on that life was a great deal more manageable if the sea could be befriended. It helped that the climate was both warm and allowed for long periods of good visibility. I once tried to use the stars on a trip in the English Channel during the month of February; it was not a high-return investment.

The low latitudes of the islands also meant that the stars rise at a steep angle. It might help to think back to the celestial sphere and how star movement is related to latitude. At the equator stars rise vertically; at the poles they move horizontally. The advantage of stars that rise steeply is that they hold the same relative bearing for longer periods. A star at the pole will move along the horizon at 15 degrees per hour, one that rises east at the equator will still be east of you three hours later.

These factors together allowed the people of the Pacific to develop a natural astro-navigation system that was very effective. It relied heavily on memory, since each navigator had to memorize a sequence of stars for each course sailed between the islands, usually from their own island to a neighboring one and then back again. As each star rose or set above or below a useful height on the horizon, so the next one would be sought out. These "star paths" would take the navigator right through the night, and some navigators could remember hundreds of these stars and the sequences that formed paths. Since each star rose and set in a different place, the horizon was divided up into a sort of "star compass." The star compass was not a physical object that could be carried around, but a way of remembering the star names and the directions they indicated, and therefore the islands that they could be used to find. Experienced navigators then used this conceptual idea to pass on their knowledge of the stars to young navigators. They would make a circle, using lumps of coral or anything else to hand. In a full circle there would be thirty-two different pieces of coral, each one representing a direction and named after the star needed to follow that course. The lump of coral that represented northeast was called "Hokulei," the Polynesian name for the star known in English as "Capella." More specifically, when Hokulei was rising it represented northeast, and when it was setting it represented northwest. This tradition continues in a small way to this day.

What the star compass achieves is to strip out one part of the Western method altogether. We might think to ourselves: "The island I want to get to is northeast of my island, therefore I need to find northeast. Which star will take me northeast?" But the star compass allowed the Pacific navigators to think, "The island I need is beneath 'rising Hokulei.' Let's go."

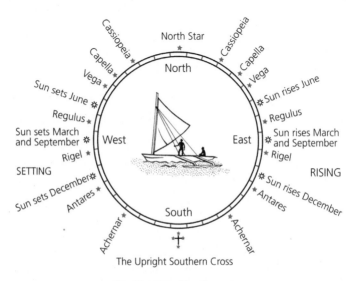

The Carolinian Star Compass.

There is nothing in the Pacific Islanders' navigational technique that is incompatible with what we now know about the celestial sphere. The differences between the two are cultural, not astronomical, since they are simply ways of conceptualizing what lies out there, beyond planet Earth. Once you are comfortable with the celestial sphere and how it works, you should find it simple to improvise or adapt to any practical system or even invent your own.

The star compass can also be used to navigate on land. If you arrive in a new town and the locals tell you there is a great restaurant three miles to the west, then you can bring the star compass and celestial sphere together by thinking of that restaurant as being one hour's walk toward the setting Orion's belt. You should be able to find it without a map, a compass, without even referring to direction itself again.

If you then decided to move to that town, you might come to know the restaurant as the "setting Orion's belt restaurant" as a way of remembering which way it is. A cafe north of the village might become the "Polaris cafe." Once all the regular destinations in the surrounding area had been allocated the stars that would take you to them, these could then be marked out in a circle using stones. You would have created a star compass for your new town.

Reading the Sea

In an unlikely chain of events the Western world learned of an indigenous method of navigation in the Pacific through coconuts, shells, a missionary, and a German naval captain.

The Reverend Luther Halsey Gulick was born in Honolulu in 1828, was educated in New England, and spent eight years in the Marshall Islands in Micronesia before being forced by ill-health to return to Honolulu. Gulick's primary interest was in the word of God, not Pacific navigation, but he could see a synergy: "Their passion for voyaging will yet facilitate the spread of the Gospel among them."

During his tour of duty, he noted the local use of coconut fibers, sticks, and shells bound together to form a chart. The extraordinary thing about this chart was that instead of focusing on the constant relationships between the islands themselves, it purported to represent the swell and waves that could be expected between those islands.

Thirty years after Gulick had flagged his discovery, a Captain Winkler of the German Navy traveled to the islands himself and somehow managed to persuade the locals to divulge their secrets. This wouldn't have been easy, since navigational knowledge in the Pacific has traditionally been considered sacred and confidential. This knowledge guaranteed an islander not only gainful employment but also an elevated position in Micronesian society. The secrets that Captain Winkler managed to uncover are the next area for the natural navigator to investigate.

The sea may not reveal much about the sun's behavior, but it can reveal a lot about what the wind has been doing. The following methods depend in part on some understanding of the prevailing wind direction in an area. This is something that locals come to know well, but as we have seen, visitors can find it from natural sources on land, such as the trees. Out at sea, it is impossible to gauge what the prevailing wind direction of an area is, only what the wind is doing and has been doing recently.

Learning to read the sea to find direction starts with an understanding of the relationship between wind and water. A gentle breeze over a pond or even a breath into a cup of tea visibly disturbs the liquid. This instant effect of wind on water creates ripples and these die down quickly as the surface tension of the water dampens them. If a wind blows more steadily and strongly over water, then the water absorbs more energy, and the ripples become waves. The size of the waves will be influenced by the wind strength, the length of time it has been blowing, and the distance it has blown across open water, known as its "fetch." On the day Marvin Creamer set out on his extraordinary voyage the sun had been stamped out by heavy black clouds, and there was a northwesterly gale blowing. He observed that the wind was blowing offshore, thereby averting the danger of being blown back on to a lee shore, and also that the waves could not have grown too large because the fetch was minimal. A gale blowing offshore can create smaller waves than a much lighter wind that has blown across hundreds of miles.

Waves move forward, carrying this new energy with them. It is tempting to think of the water moving forward, but it is the energy that the wind has given to the water that is moving, not the water itself, which is mostly only moving up and down. Think of the motion of a whip: A wave travels all the way down the whip carrying a lot of energy with it, but the whip never leaves the hand.

The energy that is carried in waves at sea can travel long distances, over 1,000 miles. When wave energy travels beyond the area where the waves were created by the wind this is called swell. Ripples, waves, and swell are all manifestations of the wind giving the water energy. There is not a scientific point when a ripple becomes a wave, or when a wave becomes swell, but there are however differences in the appearance and behavior of each.

Natural navigators are mainly interested in swell, since swell is more dependable than waves, and ripples only reveal the current wind direction, which is easy to feel anyway. Understanding swell is first about reading the patterns in the sea in open water. Reading a swell and understanding that it was generated by a known prevailing wind can reveal direction in the open sea.

Often the open sea will contain a mixture of swell and waves that can be tricky to decipher, particularly if the two are of comparable height. Waves travel in the same direction as the wind. If the wind changes, then the waves will change direction, too, superimposing themselves on a swell that has not changed direction. Swell will continue across or even against the wind. Swell tends to be less steep than waves, since all waves flatten and elongate as they travel. This is why waves sometimes break in open water but swell does not. Another effect of the greater scale of swell is that each crest and trough runs in unbroken lines. They are much wider than waves and run much farther, often appearing to stretch out into the distance.

Even with practice, identifying the difference between waves and swells can be difficult. Seasoned practitioners of this art often rely on their own physical sensations to determine what is moving beneath the boat. Lying on deck is a common method for detecting the rhythm in which the boat is moving on the swell. Balance comes into play, too, but learning to tap into the physical sensation goes further and deeper than that. This was perhaps the reason the experienced island sailor Captain Ward reported that a man's testicles were the best apparatus for assessing swell, and that this was the preferred method in the Pacific.

Anyone who has spent any time on small boats will have witnessed the skipper sticking their head above decks for no apparent reason and enquiring sternly if everything is all right. This is often prompted by a sense, perhaps a slight change in the rhythm of rolling or sounds of waves, that something has altered unexpectedly. Quite often this skipper will be unable to articulate the reason for their concern, since it will have been triggered by a subconscious monitoring of the movement of the boat through the waves and swells. This subconscious ability even pervades sleep for some old salts. I have been hollered at for coming off course by a skipper who seemed to be sound asleep. This is something that can be felt by anyone on the boat, but it tends to be the one with the responsibility for the crew's lives who is most attuned.

For some sailors a change is detected when seasickness arrives after many hours without a problem. This is because our inner ears are more sensitive to certain motions than others.

The larger the swell, the easier it is to identify and to work out the direction it is coming from, but there is a payoff between size of swell and ease of sailing conditions. I can remember being frustrated at the difficulty of reading a modest swell for several days out in the Atlantic. Then a distant storm off Madeira generated large swell that hit me. Although it was much easier to read where it was coming from, it threw the boat around so badly that I had other considerations to worry about, like trying to get around without injuring myself and struggles like getting food and water into my mouth.

Storm-generated swell is the exception, and it bullies and overrides the prevailing swell. More typically the swell will have been generated by steadier prevailing winds, often blowing over great distances undeterred and unmolested by land. Although not guaranteed, the seasonal probability of wind direction is as dependable on some oceans as anywhere on Earth, because the effect of solar heating is far more constant over a large patch of water than on land. Each ocean will have its wind trends and consequently its familiar swells, something that surfers from the Carolinas to Hawaii appreciate.

The swell, like the trees on land, reveals the direction that the wind has been blowing. If a navigator knows the direction that the swell is moving, it can be used as a compass. The swell is dependable for hours and often days at a time, but not months or years in the way that the trees are. It cannot be used in isolation for long periods. Instead it is best to check the swell direction against the sun or stars. Then if the celestial clues are lost the swell can be used to hold a course. However, when the swell is used for shaping a course it is still preferable to pick a point in the distance to aim for. The horizon is rarely completely empty, and a cloud or line in a bank of clouds will usually offer itself and work for a short period.

Swell will nearly always be used in conjunction with the wind itself as another means of holding a course. It is easier over very short periods to hold a course relative to the wind direction; there are even fantastic gizmos called wind vanes that do it for you automatically these days. However, the wind is less constant than the swell, and it is possible to sail on a constant bearing relative to wind and come wildly off course, even in theory to sail a complete circle.

The people of Micronesia have kept the art of navigating by swell alive, spending years refining it, absorbing the energy of the waves and swell, and coming to know them instinctively. But there is nothing theoretically taxing about reading swell, and the basics can be picked up easily. Even those going sailing for the first time cannot help but detect the change in rhythm and motion of a small boat as it changes course in a large swell.

Large boats give a different perspective. The deck of a passenger ferry is a good vantage point to sample patterns in the sea. On a recent summer holiday in France, we took a ferry across the English Channel, from the coastal town of Poole to St. Malo in Brittany, on the northwest French coast. This is some of the most disturbed water in the world. There are fast tides, islands and one of the busiest shipping lanes, all churning the water up and confusing the effects of wind. Yet even here it is possible to detect some patterns as the anarchy of waves overlapping waves settles near the middle of the Channel before dissolving into a mêlée again on the far side.

People in the Marshall Islands created stick charts as a physical representation of their deep understanding of swell patterns out at sea, but these charts also portray the relationship between swell and land, in particular what happened when swell came into contact with islands.

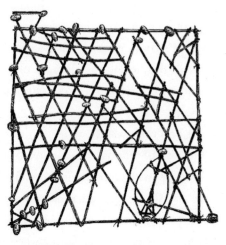

A stick chart from the Marshall Islands in the Pacific. It shows typical swell patterns and how these interacted with the islands.

When waves meet the coastline they are reflected off land in the same way that a wave will travel up and down a bath, bouncing off each end until all the energy has dissipated. The angle at which the wave reflects off land and the strength of the returning wave are determined by the incoming wave and the land it meets. Curved and gently shelving beaches will reflect much weaker waves than rock cliffs.

When a reflected wave meets an incoming wave they interfere with each other and the pattern in the water, the height, shape, and rhythm of the waves will change. This is all now well understood in terms of modern physics, but the islanders learned to read these patterns of interference at sea. They came to discern the difference between open swell, reflected swell, and the patterns of interference on each side of an island. Sometimes they could do this even in the dark, using the sensation of different wave patterns and the twinkling phosphorescence that the interference patterns generated.

It is possible to simulate these effects on a smaller scale. By blowing gently from one end of a shallow rectangular bowl of water in which there is a rock "island," it is possible to set up ripples that act as swell. By altering the strength of "wind" and position of the "island" it is possible to make out faint lines of interference in the water.

Beneath the waves and the swell the water is rarely perfectly still. If the wind blows steadily enough, then currents will be set up as the water follows the wind direction in a broad and gentle stream. Currents are also formed by differences in temperature and water density. In the Mediterranean the sun heats the water and causes evaporation. Then the water level lowers, and water tries to flow in to replace it from the Atlantic. However, the evaporation causes the Mediterranean water to have a higher concentration of salt and as a result it is more dense; as the fresher Atlantic water flows in through the Straits of Gibraltar, a deeper current of heavier, saltier water flows out below it.

The best known of the major sea currents is the Gulf Stream, which is created by the trade winds blowing across the Atlantic and flows northeast past the east coast of the United States and Newfoundland before crossing the Atlantic Ocean. The Gulf Stream has been known to navigators for centuries, having first been described by the Spanish explorer Juan Ponce de León in the sixteenth century, after which it became widely used by Spanish ships sailing from the Caribbean to Spain. Like all substantial winds and currents it is also influenced by the Coriolis force, which is caused by the Earth's spin. This force acts on everything that moves over a long distance on the Earth's surface, forcing them to the right in the northern hemisphere.

The Gulf Stream carries warm salty water at a speed of close to five knots and has a famous indigo blue color that sets it apart from the other waters and currents that it passes, being particularly noticeable at its western edge, where the clear line is known as the "Cold Wall." In the area of the Grand Banks, the submarine plateau rising from the continental shelf off Newfoundland, the warm current, meets the southerly cold Labrador current, and the mixture of warm and cold air creates one of the foggiest areas on Earth.

Sea currents, like most natural phenomena, are not isolated systems, and their influence reaches beyond the water itself. The Inca empire was fueled in part by harvesting the guano from the birds that thrived off the fish, who thrived off the plankton that thrived in the cold water that flowed north to replace the water that the Gulf Stream had taken away.

Knowledge of currents is useful not only because any boat, great or small, will be carried by them but also because in some cases they can be helpful in determining position, by drawing a line in the sea. The Kuroshio Current that flows northeast in the Pacific was observed by Captain King, who sailed on one of Cook's voyages and runs a deeper and darker blue than the water around it. In fact it is so distinct that it appears in references that date back 800 years.

The majority of currents are very hard to detect and so it is fortunate that they are weak, typically moving at less than one knot. Modern navigation relies on accumulated seasonal data, so that nearly all passages are undertaken through currents that are understood and factored in to the navigation, but that remain undetected. If a current moves a boat in the open ocean, the captain has very few natural means of detecting it. Creamer, who must have been as finely attuned to the water's signs as any modern sailor, noticed "bands of riffled water" north of the equator and identified them as equatorial countercurrents, but few sailors look out for these signals.

In the Pacific, the early Polynesians and Micronesians did not have charts and atlases complete with data about currents, so they relied on experience and a practical method that works over short distances. By knowing that a destination island was in the direction indicated by two landmarks, it was possible for the navigator to gauge and assess the current strength and direction early on in a voyage and compensate accordingly. In Tikopia, in the Solomon Islands, there is a beach that lines up with a gully running up a mountainside. The line that runs through these two features, the transit line in Western terminology, is the correct course for the island of Anuta—the beach's name is "Mataki Anuta" or "Looking on Anuta." It is used early on in a voyage to assess the current and then make the necessary adjustments.

This technique can be applied in any situation where two things clearly visible on land can be lined up. Imagine you are floating in a boat, with no engine on or sails up and in still wind conditions. In front of you a church spire is visible, lining up with a radio mast. Any change in that alignment will reveal what the water is doing beneath you. (This also happens to be an excellent technique for checking whether an anchor is holding; if the anchor drags, then the alignment, or transit line, will shift.)

Currents have managed to shape great journeys and baffle great travelers even when they are half out of the water. The Norwegian explorer Fridtjof Nansen planned to close in on the North Pole by allowing his specially reinforced ship, the *Fram*, to become frozen in the seasonal ice and letting it drift north. Locked in the ice, Nansen was unable to control the direction in which the *Fram* moved, which he found himself at a loss to understand at times:

> I cannot account for any south-going current here—there ought to be a north-going one. If the current runs south here, how is that great open sea we steamed north across to be explained? And the bay we ended in farthest north? These could only be produced by the north-going current which I presupposed.

As Nansen's experience underlines, currents cannot be easily predicted in areas unknown to the navigator. The modern navigator has the benefit of sea charts, but even so it is important to remain aware and vigilant, something that those whose lives are vulnerable to the currents have demonstrated. The Inuit's natural awareness has helped them to develop a unique technique. They have used floating kelp or "*qiqquaq*," as a guide, looking for the submerged fronds that are led away from the floating root by the currents.

The Tides

Our understanding of the tides remains imperfect, but it is an encouraging area for those who value natural skills. In 1872, the Irish mathematician and engineer Lord Kelvin built an impressive and strange machine, a contraption of dials and drums aimed at predicting the tide. Man's struggle to master this elusive natural phenomenon led to more and more complex machinery, culminating in the Fleisher-Harris tide predicting machine in 1910. Capable of juggling thirty-seven different celestial and other variables, this behemoth stood over ten feet long and nearly six feet wide, a maze of gears and levers. It was however still only able to approximate the behavior of tidal water.

Even in this age of computers that can make billions of calculations per second and beat every human being at chess, there is not a machine in the world that can accurately predict tides at a new location without the assistance of human observation. In tides nature has found a complexity to outwit the zeros and ones.

The Warao people of the Orinoco Delta in Venezuela remain blissfully unaware of such technological advancements, but they still manage to find their way by staying attuned to the tide. To do so, they carefully monitor where they are in the tide cycle. The

Delta has a tidal range between high and low waters of about six feet, and so by monitoring that and the direction of current (which is easy to spot, as there are plants that drift around on it) they can work out which direction is toward the sea and which upriver. This is their main navigational tool.

Our dangerous dance with this periodic movement of water goes back a long way. Pytheas, our old Greek friend and measurer of shadows, brought back reports that the tides in northern Europe were a very different beast than those of the Mediterranean, but it took a long time before this observation translated into anything close to their taming. In the intervening years Julius Caesar struggled with the tides off Britain's coast (Shakespeare compared the fortunes of men with their ebb and flow in his play of the same name).

Our battle with the tides has sometimes ended in great sadness: At the end of the nineteenth century a sailing ship was wrecked off the Channel Islands, a small archipelago off the French coast of Normandy. The thirty passengers, all women, managed to escape from the water by clambering on to a rock on the nearby Ecréhous to await rescue. The crew, possibly more aware of the tidal range, swam to safety on a higher ledge. Night fell as they waited for help, and the tide rose. When rescuers did finally arrive, the rock that the women had chosen was bare. Legend has it that screams can still be heard as spring tides cover the rock known as "*Prieres des Femmes.*"

Even today, the movement of the tides is fully understood by very few people in the world. For every simple line of colored lichens at a high water mark there are plenty of vexing questions. Are tides a horizontal or vertical motion of water? Why do they rise and fall only about an inch in large areas of the Mediterranean and up to more than three feet in Venice? Why does the water race past Alderney at seven knots, but at a quarter that speed a few miles away? Why do some places, like the Gulf of Mexico, have only one high tide every twenty-four hours when most places have two?

The concise answer is that the moon accounts for up to a foot of vertical movement in the oceans, the sun for up to six inches, and every other effect is caused by the reaction as a body of water moves into shallower water and the intricate complexities of coastlines. The tide races up narrow funnels like the Bristol Channel and is barely detectable in the center of the Atlantic. These are the dominant factors, but to predict an exact tidal height it is necessary to take account of numerous other factors like wind, ocean currents, and air pressure. An approximation of tidal behavior is easy, but an exact picture is much more complex. In the Gulf of Mexico the wave interference as the tidal water is reflected back from the coastline effectively cancels out one of the tides.

The moon's role in the tides has been recognized for thousands of years. The scholar-monk Venerable Bede was pouring forth accurate observations at the start of the eighth century. An Old Norse text called *Konungs skuggsjá* or the *King's Mirror*, which dates back to 1250, noted the following:

> The tide, when it rises, completes in seven days and half a
> day of the eighth day. And every seventh day there is a flood
> tide in place of ebb. The moon when it waxes, completes its
> course in sixteen days, less six hours, and in like period it
> wanes. And it is always true that at this time the flood tide is

highest and the ebb strongest. But when the moon has
waxed to half, the flood tide is lowest and the ebb, too, is
quite small.

The *Konungs skuggsjá* explains here that the tidal cycle lasts about
two weeks and the water heights and speeds are most dramatic
near full or new moon and least impressive when there is a half
moon. We now call these two extremes spring and neap tides.

Even if the science behind tides is well understood, there is
still a gulf to be crossed in terms of being able to use this knowledge for finding direction. At its most basic, this means being
aware that a high tide will follow about six hours after a low tide,
and vice versa. This can help with the planning of short trips on
coastal land or with the timing over shallow entrances to harbors.
This logic works with the flow, too: If the tidal water is flowing fast
in one direction there is a very good chance that it will be flowing
fast in the other direction six hours hence. It is possible to refine
this understanding. Tidal flow roughly follows something known
as the "Rule of Twelfths." Starting at either end of the tidal cycle,
low or high, in the first hour one twelfth of the water will flow; in
the second hour, two twelfths; in the third, three twelfths; in the
fourth, three twelfths; in the fifth, two twelfths; and in the sixth
and final hour, one twelfth. Put a simpler way, half the water flows
through in the middle two hours, so this is when the greatest rate
of both water flow and change in tidal height should be expected.
Shortly after a full moon you can be guaranteed a very high tide
about six hours after a very low one. Similarly, if the moon is full
or new do not head out halfway between low and high tide if you
wish to avoid fast-moving tidal water.

Another aspect to using the tides comes about through understanding the relationship between moon phase and tide. Sometimes this can be used more for fun than navigation. On holiday on a tidal beach, if you see a half moon in the sky, the tide will not reach anywhere near its high-water mark, which means that there will be great swaths of beach that nobody is daring to lie on below this mark. These broad strips of prime sand are ripe for colonization by wily natural navigators and should be seized upon as a prize for not having found your way to the beach by computer.

Color

A cupful of sea water is not blue. The color of the sea is partly influenced by the reflection of the colors of the sky. But the water also absorbs some of the red end of the light spectrum. The combined effect is that we perceive the sea as blue. The effect of the sky's light can be seen most clearly during sunny days as small fair-weather cumulus clouds cast shadows on the surface of the sea, giving patches of it a moodier appearance and reducing its blueness. This effect does not provide any navigational help. For that we look elsewhere.

Under identical light, not all sea colors are the same. As with the Gulf Stream and Kuroshio Current with their dark blue waters, differences abound. Color changes and contrasts can be caused by silt carried in rivers. Herodotus noted that the Nile discolored the water more than fifty miles from its mouth, and the Amazon carries sediment from its 1,100 tributaries out to sea, giving the sea water near its mouth a muddy yellow appearance.

Aristotle believed that the sea's saltiness was caused by the Earth sweating. Another way of looking at it might be to describe the sea as a weak solution of almost everything on Earth. Either way, when it comes to the color of the sea, the broadest effect is caused by differences in levels of salt in the water and the impact this has on microorganic life in the sea. The higher the salt content, the harder it is for tiny creatures like phytoplankton to thrive. Phytoplankton are the very broad base of the ocean's food pyramid, supporting almost all other marine life, and they are sensitive to environmental changes like salinity levels. Where there is a gradual change, like the meeting of fresh water and brackish water, this can sometimes be seen dramatically, because a plankton bloom colors the water vividly but then tails away as the salt levels rise.

The general effect usually determines how blue or green the sea is: blue where it is very salty and green where salt levels are low. The Mediterranean is very salty and consequently low in phytoplankton, which gives it a rich blue color. In the Arctic and Antarctic the seas are constantly diluted by fresh water melting from the ice and so organisms thrive, giving the polar waters a signature greenness. This was noted by the Japanese explorer Nobu Shirase during his expedition to the Antarctic in 1910:

> The sea was fortunately clear of ice, and as we looked about us we were surrounded by the rippling greasy blue-green waters so characteristic of the Ross Sea.

There is another major factor in sea color: water depth. During Marvin Creamer's voyage, he was delighted to spot a change of sea color from blue to green off the coast of New Zealand. The color change in this instance was being caused by a change in depth as his boat passed over the continental shelf. Creamer knew that the shelf is not wide off New Zealand and so realized that this color change heralded that the New Zealand coastline was near.

It helps to understand the effect of the ground on the color of water. The simple rule is that shallowing brings change, but it is possible to refine this. As blue water shallows over yellow sand, the colors will change as gradually as the sea floor rises from dark blue to blue-green, then to green and finally to yellow, by which point you are aground. The same effect but with different colors will be found over white or black sand. The pioneering Australian navigator Harold Gatty, who spent some of his later years living on his own Pacific island, was able to navigate at speed through uncharted reefs using this method.

In the bas-reliefs of boats from ancient Egypt, dating back over 4,000 years, there stands a man with a sounding pole at the bow. The pole would be lowered until it met the ground, giving the crew a constant and physical reading of water depth. Odysseus carried a long pole aboard his ship, and there are times for all sailors when such an instrument, possibly the first ever invented, might seem like a far better solution than modern electronics. To this day it is good practice to carry a lead line, a weight on a string, which can be used to determine your depth of water with no batteries, software, or electricity plug attached to it.

The technique of adding tallow to the end of a weight gave this simple method a dimension that the echo sounder still lacks, which was the ability to sample the seabed itself to gather clues to location. Herodotus, when commenting that the Nile was discoloring the sea, also noted that the mud causing this could be brought up on a line when still a day's sail from land. The seabed is varied, with mud in places and rock, shells, or weed in others, which is useful for contemporary mariners who are searching for a good spot to drop an anchor where it will hold but not get snarled. Local knowledge of this kind was used for years before charts, as a clue to the proximity of land. It was by taking soundings that the crew of St. Paul's boat realized that trouble was imminent, the depth dropped from twenty to fifteen fathoms as they were driven toward a lee shore and shipwreck.

The Birds

Climbing out of the water for a few moments and casting our eyes upward, we find feathered navigational indicators, or birds. The historical relationship between birds and nautical navigation is strong. Captive birds have been used on board ships to sight land for as long as records exist. Birds, including doves, ravens, and a swallow, appear in the ancient epic of Gilgamesh and in the Genesis account of Noah and the Flood. Pliny the Elder refers to this method being used by sailors in the area of modern-day Sri Lanka in the first century AD. According to Norse legend, the second person to land on Iceland was Flóki Vilgerðarson, who took three ravens with him on his voyage and released one at a time as he felt he was drawing closer to land. The first two returned, but the third continued onward, and Flóki followed its lead to Iceland. He earned himself the nickname "Raven Flóki" for posterity.

Throughout history, the sighting of wild birds has been tied to an understanding of where land is, each area having its particular residents, such as the frigate birds off the Seychelles. Cosmas, also known as Indicopleustes—he who sailed to India—was an Egyptian who had a very good reason for wanting to be sure where land was: He firmly believed that the Earth was flat and that it had four corners. Writing in the sixth century, he describes seeing a flock of birds: "A great flock, all the time, of the birds called Souspha followed us, flying generally high over our heads, and the presence of these was a sign that we were near the ocean." The ocean to Cosmas was the edge of the world.

It is rare that contemporary seagoers find animals as noteworthy as our ancestors did, but it is not surprising to discover that Marvin Creamer writes of them: "We are seeing more prions and fewer Albatrosses and wonder if this could be an indication that we are nearing Tasmania."

The modern sailor, perhaps already familiar with the sight of fulmars heading home at dusk, but wishing to glean more navigational information from the birds, needs to take note of several factors. These include species, number, frequency, time, season, and behavior. It is a vast subject but, with a little diligent observation, birds can assist the natural navigator.

Species is the place to start, because if individual birds can be identified, and their habits are known, then some general conclusions about location can be drawn. Flocks of birds are much more significant than individual birds, since solitary birds can be as eccentric as individual people, but it is unlikely that a flock of birds will collectively behave in a way contrary to their usual habits.

It helps to be able to recognize a few of the likely suspects in each area and these can be discovered by talking to locals and reading up a little on the natural history of any new area before going to sea. The most common nautical clue that birds give is their distance from land. The first distinction to be made here is between coastal and pelagic birds. The latter, such as petrels and albatrosses, are oceanic birds, able to sustain themselves for long periods in the open sea, and therefore offer very few clues to location. Coastal birds are more anchored to the land and so their habits can help the navigator. Coastal birds have different comfortable ranges from land, larger birds tending to roam farther. The terns and noddies are found up to about twenty-five miles from land, boobies up to fifty miles and the frigate bird farther still, perhaps seventy-five miles. In other words, if you are in a life raft and see a frigate bird on day one, a pair of boobies on day two, and a flock of terns on day three you can get your drinks order ready. If they appear in the opposite order, you might want to consider which of your companions to eat first.

The behavior of birds is worth noting because it is sometimes possible to identify birds from their behavior even if you have no idea what they look like. The frigate bird, for example, has evolved an unusual lifestyle because it is not very fond of getting wet—its feathers do not cope with water as well as the birds that like to fish. Consequently it harasses, bullies, and steals for its food. It can be identified from this antisocial behavior by a navigator who has long forgotten what it looks like.

Thomas Gladwin, an anthropologist who spent time researching this subject with indigenous Pacific Island navigators, noticed some very distinct traits in different birds. He remarked that a white tern with a fish sideways in its beak was invariably heading for land, likely with a takeaway too substantial to finish at sea. A booby would commonly circle any boat that it passed over, making as if to land on it, but then continuing on toward land as at dusk. Tropic birds would nest on land, but often left their return until very late, even well after dark, while the plover only ranged up to ten miles from land and could be identified by the trademark "coo-ling, coo-ling" sounds that they made.

Since most coastal birds like to set out in the morning and return to land at night, it is fair to assume that a flock of such birds heading in a uniform direction at dusk are likely indicating the direction of land.

Strange Ways

The more time a navigator spends at sea, the more unusual the observations become. These observations can lead to methods that are specific to each region, and while they might not all be transferable to other parts of the world, they are no less fascinating for it.

The navigator and writer David Lewis spent many months researching navigation in the Pacific and documented some unusual methods of reading the sea that he witnessed during his time there. One of these is the use of luminescence, or phosphorescence as it is more commonly called. This is not the omnipresent twinkling caused by chemical reactions in small organisms, but a distinctly different and much less well understood phenomenon that resembles "underwater lightning," typically about a yard below the surface and roughly ninety-five miles from an

island. The extraordinary and valuable thing about these flashes
and streaks of light is that they appear to emanate from the direction of an island and are still used by local sailors to steer by on
nights with rain and poor visibility. The phenomenon has not yet
been fully explained, but Lewis believed that it may be caused by
a deep swell movement or possibly reflected swell.

Lewis also met an island navigator by the name of Abera
Beniata of Nikunau in Kiribati, who claimed that there is an
effective method of using the sun's rays. Near the middle of the
day, when the sun is almost overhead, if the navigator peers down
into the water the sun's rays will not appear uniform. There will
be long rays and short rays visible in the water, and the shorter
rays will indicate the direction of land.

If all of these methods seem logical and not strange enough,
then perhaps it is worth considering a method described by
Makea Nui Ariki, High Chieftainess of Rarotonga. In 1965 she
proclaimed that if an eyelash can be plucked easily, then land
is near.

Landfall

Making landfall is one of the times when the risk of wrecking
increases and so the navigator must be alert to all the assistance
that nature can offer. It is fortunate, therefore, that where land
and sea meet animal and plant life, light, air, and water all behave
in particular ways.

Landfall is not the moment of touching land, but of sighting
it. Knowing this helps solve a riddle that has puzzled many. It
does not matter how you travel: by foot, boat or car, there always

seems to be a discrepancy between the navigator's estimated time of arrival and the time it actually takes to get there. All of us have a childhood memory of repeating, ad infinitum, "Are we there yet?" The word "landfall" is the key to explaining this. The navigator is focused on the moment when arrival at our destination is within sight or near guaranteed, since this represents the final hurdle in *finding* a destination. In the case of driving this might be a signpost to a small village, when walking it might be rejoining a known footpath that leads home, and at sea it is the moment when land comes into sight: the landfall. There is always then a small journey still to be made from this moment to actual physical arrival: the turning of a key, dropping of a backpack, or tying of a knot.

The dangers of sailing close to an unknown coastline mean that it has been common practice since ancient times for maritime visitors to employ the assistance of "pilots," mariners with intimate knowledge of the local hazards. It is an unnatural process for any captain to hand over control of their vessel, and some customs have evolved to cope with this. In ancient times these customs were typically blunt; the pilot had a coveted job that guaranteed a good income and a place at the heart of maritime activity, but it was not without its burdens. If the pilot placed the ship in danger, then they could be executed by the sailors, "without ceremony."

Local knowledge was protected by the pilots but it did find its way into written form, and by the fifth century BC we have the earliest known compilation of sailing directions in the Periplus of Scylax of Caryanda, which listed details about harbors in the Mediterranean among other nautical tidbits.

Nautical folklorist Horace Beck recounts an amusing tale about the use of pilots in the Pentland Firth, which separates the Orkney Islands from the northernmost point of mainland Scotland. A British admiral once insisted that a pilot use the appropriate nautical chart to do his job. The pilot answered that he was not keen on the idea, since the chart made it appear as though there were too many wrecks in the area.

Landmarks have always been used as navigational tools. Here is a neat example of how the details were remembered in Newfoundland:

> When Joe Bett's P'int you is abreast
> Dave's Rock bears due west
> West-nor'west you must steer
> Till Brimstone Head do appear
>
> The Tickle's narrer, not very wide
> The deepest water's on the starboard side
> When in the harbor you is shot
> Four fathoms you is got.

One method that is used in the search for land is the scouring of the sky for anomalous clouds. Clouds often form over land by the orographic effect, which is when the landmass pushes moist maritime air higher, causing it to condense and form clouds. This is why the windward side of a mountain range exposed to moist maritime air can experience very heavy rainfall, while the downwind side is often drier, since it sits in a "rain shadow."

Clouds can also be used to find low lying islands by looking for a different meteorological effect. The sun heats the land more quickly than water, and warm air will rise in a column above the island, again causing the moist air to condense and form a cloud. A solitary stationary cloud, or even better one that remains motionless over the horizon as others pass it by, is likely to be sitting atop an island. If the warm air is rising vigorously enough it can both form a cloud and then carve it in two, creating a telltale pair of clouds that resemble eyebrows.

It is not only the existence and shape of clouds that can yield clues to the whereabouts of land, but their color. If the color contrast between land and sea is striking, then sometimes this can be seen on the underside of a cloud, a green tinge above a Pacific lagoon, for example.

The natural friction between land and sea can yield clues in the form of flotsam. Pieces of wood and, sadly, rubbish can appear anywhere in the ocean, but the incidence of these sightings tends to increase with proximity to land. There is one notable exception to this rule. Where currents are weak or converge there are often stagnant waters, creating ideal conditions for some life-forms such as the eponymous weed that can be found in the Sargasso Sea. Unfortunately these waters also act as graveyards for floating detritus that gathers in giant, slowly swirling zones of trash floating in the ocean. The giant "garbage patch" created by the North Pacific Gyre is estimated to be larger than Texas.

Our senses, as always, are what make natural navigation possible. Our eyes might detect a change in the water or the smallest of clouds in the sky. The sound of breakers has acted as a warning signal since the first nautical journeys. The feel of the waves and swell, or even a slight change in the wind, can be used to shape a course. I will never forget the sweet, fragrant and lightly spiced smell of St. Lucia in the Caribbean after my first Atlantic crossing.

Underwater

Navigating naturally underwater is not as foreign as it sounds, at least not down to a certain depth. The same sun will penetrate shallow clear water and even give clues from shadows. It is also possible to use moonlight at night.

No diver is safe without a good idea of depth, and instruments are the safe way to monitor this, but light levels provide nature's best supporting evidence. It takes time to become familiar with the differences in underwater light. Both sun and moonlight are refracted by the water, and so a lot of light is lost when the light hits the water from low in the sky, in the early mornings and late afternoons in the case of the sun.

The seabed has a topography in the same way that dry land does, and the underwater natural navigator must be just as finely attuned to it. A diver can follow valleys, trenches, and vertical drops in much the same way as the navigator on land.

Just as land that slopes down may indicate the direction of the sea, so the opposite can be true close to the shoreline underwater. The character of the seabed near land can also contain clues. As the water shallows, the wave action in the water creates ripples in the sand that run parallel to the shoreline. The tops of these ripples of sand will tend to be pushed over in the direction of the shore, like frozen waves.

If the waves are strong, then close to where they break they meet water that is moving in the opposite direction, having been reflected from the shore. This can create diamond shaped ripples in the sand.

The most dependable underwater technique is the same as the first one we become comfortable with on land: recognizing landmarks. Some of the landmarks may be unique to the underwater environment, like coral pillars or kelp beds, but a few will be strangely familiar, such as submerged trees and even cars. So long as an object is unlikely to be confused with another and will not be moved by tides or currents, then it will serve as a landmark.

Underwater plants can reveal direction in the same way as land ones. They grow up toward the light, but this effect may be negligible when compared to the way they are combed by the currents. Instead of a prevailing wind, it will be a current that leaves its mark. The large coastal seaweeds, like kelp, are swept in line with the current, whereas the purple corals, known as sea fans, will be at right angles to this current to maximize feeding and respiration rates.

For all that we have come to rely on modern instruments to assist us, the art of natural navigation is far from dead. In some places, like the Pacific, it is enjoying a small but healthy renaissance at the hands of groups like the excellent Polynesian Voyaging Society. The Society has been undertaking voyages since 1973 as a means of keeping Polynesian maritime culture and heritage alive with local island communities.

A philosophy of keeping the senses alive to the water and elements can only be a positive influence on any sea journey. The sea has always attracted those with a broad, holistic view of the world and even those who go to sea for long periods without this view often come back with it.

CHAPTER 6

The Elements

Nearly all journeys undertaken by humankind take place within the thin layer of gases that lies between space and the surface of our planet. The Earth's atmosphere is not static, but is in constant motion as weather systems and winds whirl about above the surface of the Earth. The weather can influence the travel experience, but it can also be used by the natural navigator.

Seen from the surface, the dynamic change that constitutes the weather takes place against a background of a blue or black sky. One of the simplest of questions, asked by small children the world over, took a surprisingly long time to answer: Why is the sky blue?

The color of the sky would no doubt have featured around the table at the X Club, a private Victorian dining club with nine scientist members. One of them was John Tyndall, an eminent physicist who helped us to understand concepts like the greenhouse effect and why some animals, like peacocks, appear blue. He also demonstrated how light was scattered by molecules in the atmosphere.

There is a relationship between the wavelength of light and the amount it will be scattered by air molecules. The sun's light that hits our atmosphere consists of different wavelengths. Blue light has a relatively short wavelength compared to the red light at the other end of the visible spectrum. Short-wavelength light scatters more than long-wavelength light, meaning that blue light is scattered much more than red light. Wherever we look in the sky, other than at the sun itself, the light we see must be the light scattered as it enters the Earth's atmosphere. It is strange to think that without an atmosphere, the daytime sky would look like the star-studded nighttime one, but with a fiery ball moving across it.

This scattering of light is also the reason for the yellows, oranges, and reds of sunrises and sunsets. The sun's light is having to pass through so much more of the Earth's atmosphere at the start and end of the day, and so the blue light is scattered out altogether, leaving the less easily scattered colors at the other end of the spectrum, reds and yellows. This scattering effect is also influenced by airborne particles such as pollutants. There are usually more pollutants in the atmosphere at the end of a day than at its start. These additional particles scatter out even more light from the blue end of the spectrum and the result is that sunsets look subtly different from sunrises; west and east look different, although spotting this in photographs is a challenge.

The shades of blue in the sky are shaped by the air itself, its density, its humidity, and the level of pollutants. The sky often appears darker from the tops of mountains or when the air is particularly dry. Air clarity has been used for centuries as a way of predicting weather. In Polynesia, the way stars twinkle has been used to forecast rain and wind. We can now surmise that the twinkling of the stars was influenced by thin cirrus cloud high in the atmosphere, a typical sign of the leading edge of a frontal system.

In the confines of his cabin, Marvin Creamer used one small puff of humid air to draw some larger navigational conclusions:

> For the first time we saw the vapor of our breath condense
> in the cabin. Cold air from north could not have originated
> over the ocean. Its source had to be from land and in the
> high sun period of the year it could not have originated over
> anything but very high land, i.e., mountains, in all
> probability snow-covered mountains.

The nineteenth-century French physicist François Arago wrote, "Whatever may be the progress of the sciences, never will observers who are trustworthy and careful of their reputations venture to foretell the weather." Weather forecasting is a much derided science to this day because it remains so inexact. This is because while the weather is governed by easily determined factors such as air pressure, humidity, and temperature, the system is so complex that a slight error in a reading of the data can quickly become compounded and lead to an inaccurate forecast. Given that meteorologists with access to some of the world's most powerful computers are regularly confounded, one might wonder what advantage the natural navigator could gain by attempting to read the weather.

Weather is an important part of the journey. It cannot be divorced from the outdoors experience and nor should it be. For pure natural navigation purposes, however, the weather that is arriving in a few hours or days is of less interest than what is happening in the present—and also what took place in the past. Grasses are bent by the winds of the previous hours, trees by that of the past years, and the walker can use both of these while simultaneously feeling the breeze on one side of the face. The waves and swell of the sea reflect what is happening and what has happened, not what *will* happen.

The Wind

As we have seen, the wind holds an important place in the navigator's world. The sun, never far from consideration, is the prime mover of the wind. Solar energy heats the Earth's surface according to the angle of the sun's rays. Landmasses heat more quickly than the sea, creating warmer air masses. This in turn affects the air's pressure—warmer air expands, creating low pressure, while cooler air forms areas of higher pressure. The atmosphere is in perpetual motion as high pressure air tries to move into lower pressure areas. This creates wind.

The Earth's spin means that the winds never move in straight lines over long distances; the effect of the Coriolis force makes them curve around the high and low pressure systems, leading to the trademark cyclonic whirls that satellites capture and meteorologists like to prognosticate from.

There is a temptation to think of the weather as random, but of course it is not. The warmth of the sun is very regular, the landmasses do not change substantially, so it is inevitable that consistent patterns emerge. At the most obvious level, areas that get the least solar heating, like the poles, remain cold, and the tropics are consistently hot. Dependable patterns emerge at a more specific level, on both a small and large scale.

One large pattern, with great significance for Atlantic sailors, is the Azores high pressure system in the subtropical North Atlantic, which follows the sun north in the summer. The winds rotate clockwise out of the system creating the northeast to easterly trade winds that have carried transatlantic sailors from the Canary Islands to the Caribbean for centuries. The winds drive steady currents, too, and it is often said that if you throw a bottle in the sea at the Canary Islands, you will find it washed up in the Caribbean in due course. The winds of lower latitudes are generally steadier than those at higher latitudes.

South of the trade winds are the notorious doldrums of the Intertropical Convergence Zone and north of the trade winds lie the horse latitudes, supposedly named after the horses that the Spanish forced off their ships into the sea when light airs delayed their voyages and led to water shortages.

The global weather system becomes slightly more complex when there are other influencing factors. Norway and Sweden are not nearly as cold as other areas of a similar high latitude, like southern Greenland, because of the warm Gulf Stream.

Wind direction is something that causes confusion. The convention, which a lot of people find counterintuitive, is for winds to be named after the direction that they have come *from* rather than the direction in which they are blowing. A northerly wind is heading south but has come from the north. Winds bring weather with them, but, as Creamer demonstrated with his breath, they are also imbued with characteristics from the areas they pass over. It has always been useful to know what a wind might be bringing with it as well as where it will end up. The explorer Frederick Cook was one of the first to write about the importance of this at high latitudes:

> In this shiftless sea of ice, everything depends upon the wind.
> If it is south, we have steady, clear, cold weather. If it is north
> we have a warm, humid air with snow and unsettled weather. If
> it is east or west it brings a tempest with great quantities of
> driving snow; but it never ceases blowing. It is blow, blow, from
> all points of the compass. It is because of the importance of
> the wind, because it is the key-note to the day which follows,
> that our first question in the morning is "How is the wind?"

Although written over a hundred years ago, Frederick Cook's words are very modern, in the sense that he is aware the direction that the wind is coming from and the character it will therefore have. The ancient view often came from the opposite perspective, using the senses to analyze the wind's characteristics and then using that knowledge in turn to deduce the direction from which it came.

The direction of the wind might signal the daily fluctuations in weather, but it can also be used to detect broader seasonal changes, particularly in parts of the world with differing prevailing wind directions over the course of the year. A monsoon system is the most vivid example of this. Monsoons are winds that reverse direction in a seasonal cycle, often bringing much needed precipitation to areas that have endured months of hot dry weather. In these parts of the world, like sub-Saharan Africa and southern Asia, wind direction is given a lot of attention at the change of the seasons, as the search for moisture intensifies.

For ancient sailors, who were unable to sail straight into the wind, it was crucial that they followed the right wind in order to reach their destination. Pliny the Elder described the French wind of Circius as the one that would take a sailor from Narbonne (on the far southern coast of France) far across the Ligurian Sea to Ostia, near the port of Rome. Elsewhere, we find this method combined with distance to paint a more complete picture of the journey: "From Carpathus is fifty miles with Africus to Rhodes." Here Africus is the west-southwest wind that is needed to make the east-northeast journey from Carpathus to Rhodes.

There is another more fundamental reason for the importance of knowledge of the winds in earlier times. Prior to the compass, winds and their different characteristics were used to understand direction itself. The ancient Greeks noted that the south wind was dry and hot when it came from the direction of the winter sunrise (a little north of southeast) and moist and hot when it came from the direction of the winter sunset (a little north of southwest). The direction a wind had come from and the wind itself were one and the same, so that the cold northerly wind was called Boreas, a word also used to mean north.

In Athens there is a building from the first century BC called the Tower of the Winds, which beautifully demonstrates the holistic ancient view of the elements. The tower is an octagon and on each face there is a frieze depicting the wind from that direction. Boreas for north, joined by Kaikas, Eurus, Apeliotes, Notus, Livas, Zephyrus, and Skiron in the northwest, as you move round 45 degrees each time. Skiron was named after the mountains to the northwest of Athens. There were also sundials on its sides and the Tower once contained a water clock for telling the time when the sun was not shining. There stands, in one compact stone temple, testament to the meeting of wind, water, and sun. Knowledge of the eight winds led to the development of the so-called "wind rose" or "wind compass," a name which is a little misleading. The wind compass was a way of recording information about the winds themselves, it did not of itself divine direction. It was the ancestor of the compass rose that can be found in the corner of historical and some modern charts. The wind compass was the logical step for people who relied heavily on the wind's direction, but had few independent ways of checking what that direction was. The different winds, their temperature, humidity, and even the colors they brought, in the case of countries within range of the Saharan sand, all came to be closely tied to direction.

The characteristics of different winds can still be used to understand the relationship between the elements and direction. If the temperature or general feel of the wind changes, there is a good chance that the direction it is coming from has also changed. Next time you encounter what feels like an unseasonably cold or bitter wind, it is worth checking to see if it is coming from a direction other than the prevailing one. In certain places this can lead to smells that are associated with certain weathers. In the UK, for example, the coldest winds tend to come from between north and east, so if there is something to the northeast that emits a distinct smell, like the sea, its smell may give a clue to wind direction and even signal in winter that snow is on its way.

Since the wind brings the weather with it, there is a strong relationship between direction and the weather itself. The simplest way of reading this is to be aware that a sudden change in wind direction will likely be accompanied by a sudden change in weather. If you remain aware of wind direction you will quickly come to notice these trends. Small shifts in wind direction throughout the day are quite common, but substantial changes usually herald a broader change in the elements. The only time I can recall a strong breeze changing through a full 180 degrees in a short space of time I also watched a blue sky disappear behind dark clouds and rain. The reason for this can be found in the relationship between the high and low pressure systems, which bring new weather fronts with them.

A weather front is the boundary separating two masses of air of different temperature and density. A cold low pressure front is leading a wedge of cold air behind it. The diagram below shows a typical low pressure frontal system and the wind directions that shift with each passing of a front.

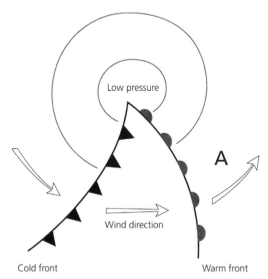

A low pressure system, with a warm and cold front, in the northern hemisphere.

Imagine that you are standing at point A in the illustration on the previous page. As the system passes you would typically experience the following changes. As the warm front approached and then passed over you, high wispy cirrus clouds would be followed by a high thin white layer of cirrostratus, thickening as it was replaced by altostratus and then a big heavy nimbostratus blanket would cover the sky as a steady rain begins to fall. The wind would veer from southwest to west as the warm front passed, and the temperature would rise. Then, as the cold front approaches the wind would veer to the northwest, the clouds would become more vertical and turbulent, the temperature would drop, and heavy downpours and thunderstorms would be likely.

Winds blowing over an ocean will be marshaled only by the pressure and temperature gradients, but over land a compromise has to be reached with the land itself. Over broad flat plains the wind can march on regardless, but as soon as the land rises up the wind cannot ignore it and must find some way to accommodate it, as Apsley Cherry-Garrard discovered:

> When crossing the undulations which ran down out of the mountain into the true pressure ridges on our right we found that the wind which came down off the mountain struck along the top of the undulation, and flowing each way, caused a N.E. breeze on one side and a N.W. breeze on the other.

In the short term the land always wins, but over many years the wind has a great advantage. It is in limitless supply, unlike the hills and mountains. The wind will often enlist the help of other elements like water in the form of rain or snow, as in the Palouse area of Washington state. Here the winter southwest winds bring snow, smoothing the southwestern inclines, but piling up in drifts on the northeastern sides. The cumulative effect of this has been to make the southwestern sides of the hills much shallower than the steep northeastern ones, a clue that can be used long after the snows have departed.

Knowing the prevailing wind direction of any location is, as stated earlier, an important and useful consideration. The windward side of a hill will show greater weathering and erosion, while the leeward side is where small particles like sand, snow, dust and leaves may accumulate. Once the patterns of the wind are understood, observations of weathering, or the lee effect, can be used to work back to the prevailing direction and lead to useful deductions. I once noticed a long thin line of dried broken leaves from the past season's corn crop on one side of a ridge at the edge of a field. The small pieces of brown leaves and husks had dropped out of the wind on the leeward side of the ridge and gathered in a neat row. A line drawn from the leaves through the ridge pointed toward the prevailing wind direction, which was southwest.

Navigators who wish to use the wind to find their way directly quickly become aware of a curious dichotomy. The wind is one of the least reliable clues in terms of consistency, yet it is one of the last natural clues to desert the senses. The best way to stay in tune with the wind is to use the senses of touch and hearing. Close your eyes and turn your head until you feel the breeze equally on both cheeks, and hear the buffeting sound equally in each ear. Having established when you are looking into the wind, raise an arm and point dead ahead, then open your eyes and look for a distant landmark. This landmark will help identify an accurate direction for the wind and serve as a reminder for as long as it is visible.

A common experience for those in the early stages of navigating with nature on land is not one of bewilderment and confusion, but complacency. Many are pleasantly surprised by how easily and quickly they are finding their way. They are equally aghast at how difficult things can quickly become when the clues start to disappear behind trees and slopes. A classic scenario involves moving from the top of a hill under clear skies with good views of the surrounding country and the sun, down into a dense wood a few minutes later with no sight of anything beyond fifty feet. In this situation even a light breeze through the trees can provide vital reassurance and renewed confidence. It may not offer pinpoint accuracy, but it is a start. However, there is not much point in asking the wind for help when it has been ignored for hours. If it has been acknowledged early on in the journey, its direction checked and compared with other clues, then it will happily repay this respect long after the sun, trees, and topography have gone silent.

Every sailor must remain constantly aware of the wind direction relative to their boat. Sails that are set perfectly for one direction relative to the wind, or "point of sail," will be rendered useless when the wind shifts significantly in any direction. One of the most common ways in which a pleasant sail is transformed into a life-threatening situation is when a skipper becomes too casual about a wind coming from astern. When a wind shifts (or the boat's stern moves) from one side of the stern to the other, the boat may "jibe," meaning that the wind will move from behind one side of the mainsail to behind the other. If you have not experienced this, then imagine the moment a strong wind catches one side of an open door and slams it violently shut. Under controlled conditions this is all part of the sailing process, but an accidental jibe can move the boom across the boat with speeds and forces that would make a baseball bat to the head seem like a good alternative to anyone in the way.

The sailor is therefore aware of the importance of holding a course by keeping the boat on the same point of sail. A problem can arise if the wind direction shifts very gradually, so that it is barely perceptible. A sudden change in wind direction is unlikely and will nearly always be accompanied by other telltale changes in the weather such as squalls, but gradual shifts are common. For this reason the experts in navigating naturally using the wind, the Pacific Islanders, have learned the importance of constantly referring to other clues, such as sun, stars, and swell. The Motu people of Papua New Guinea used a particular technique to hold a course relative to both wind and a steering star. A long staff with a bark or feather pennant suspended at one end was held in line with the star and then tied in position. Any change in the canoe's heading relative to either the wind or the star could be quickly picked up by looking along this wonderful contraption called a *kino kino*.

The winds discussed thus far are those caused by large weather systems, but there are also local winds that a natural navigator must be familiar with. Land and sea breezes are caused by differences in the effect of the sun heating coastal land and the neighboring sea. Land heats up more quickly during the day than water, while the air above land also rises in temperature and expands relative to the air over the neighboring sea. The warmer air cannot expand out to sea because the air there is cooler and denser, and it cannot expand outward across the land because that air is warming and expanding also. Instead it rises and expands upward, which leaves an area of low pressure in its place. This pressure gradient leads to cool dense air from over the sea moving in over the land, creating a "sea breeze." At night the land cools more quickly than the sea, and the process is reversed, as the winds blow from land to sea.

Mountains not only shape winds that pass over them, but can also create winds of their own. If the mountain is being warmed by the sun, then the air will begin to expand and rise up the surface of the mountain. This creates upflowing air currents known as anabatic winds. If the surface of the mountain is cooler than the surrounding air (for example, if it is covered in snow), then the air will become cooler and denser and begin to fall. This leads to downward katabatic winds.

Some katabatic winds have their own names and reputations. The Bora, from the ancient Greek word "Boreas" (meaning north), is a cold fierce wind that blows down from the Alps in the north-northeast into Italy, Slovenia, and Croatia. It has been known to knock people over and even overturn cars.

The Mistral wind that blows from the northwest or north down through the Rhone Valley in France is even more notorious. It is caused by pressure systems, the katabatic effect, and a funneling effect as it works its way through the valley.

The Föhn wind, which blows from the Mediterranean, is a fierce southerly that loses its maritime moisture on the cold slopes of the Alps and then rolls down into the leeward valleys as a warmer, very dry wind. It is reputed to have a psychological impact on the people of the Foreland area in Austria, with the incidence of accidents rising in the days before the wind arrives.

The reputations of these particular winds precede them and they are unlikely to go unnoticed, but the natural navigator must also be attuned to the gentler breezes that run off more modest hills and across beaches. The key is to remain aware of the wind direction and the weather more generally, even when they are not the primary means of navigating, and to tie observations of its direction to other clues in the sky, land or water. The wind so often lives on even as the other signposts die away. It will live on even as we finish our longer journey. In the words of the bushmen of the Kalahari Desert: "When we die, the wind blows away our footprints, and that is the end of us."

The Clouds

Clouds never really exist in any static sense. They are in fact defined by their fluid shape and appearance, but they can reveal much about the character of the air and its movement, like leaves in a stream.

The sun heats water, which evaporates, whereupon the warm, moist air rises and expands. It cools as it expands, and since cool air holds less water vapor than warm air, there comes a point where the air becomes saturated, and the water condenses to form a cloud. Depending on the air temperature, which in turn is related to altitude, this visible moisture will be either water droplets or ice crystals. The exact form of a cloud will be determined by the meeting of almost all the factors that influence the atmosphere: the action of the sun, moon, water, land, air, and human and animal activity. There is not a human or computer in the world that can predict the exact shape of the clouds we will see in an hour's time.

For most people, with the exception of artists, poets, and writers like Gavin Pretor-Pinney, founder of The Cloud Appreciation Society, examination of the clouds is usually confined to looking at the broad types, since these reflect current and to a lesser extent future weather conditions.

Clouds can be used to give the observer a map of the stability of the invisible air. A blue field filled with a horizontal line of woolly sheep stretching as far as the eye can see indicates stable air and fair weather. A tall vertical cloud must be caused by unstable, rapidly rising air and will herald unsettled, possibly stormy conditions. For the natural navigator, shapes are more useful than understanding meteorological terms, and when combined with an understanding of wind direction can be used quite effectively to give short-term forecasts. A constant wind and no vertical movement in the clouds promises more settled conditions than a wind that has just shifted noticeably and a horizon of jostling giants.

Longer term weather forecasting comes with both experience and an ability to identify the individual cloud types. It is hard to predict beyond the next few hours by observing a single cloud type, but a succession of different ones can give a fuller picture. Hence a cirrus cloud that in isolation may not mean much will, if followed by others such as cirrostratus and altostratus, usually presage the arrival of a front. Many different travelers have observed this early warning while also detecting subtle changes in visibility. Gretel Ehrlich, the American writer and frequenter of Greenland, noted during a dog sled trip with a local hunter that a ring circling the sun in the morning signaled bad weather.

The next thing to consider is the direction of the wind you can feel and the direction in which the clouds appear to be moving. For the navigator there are two general levels of clouds and three levels of wind: the wind that can be felt on the ground, the wind at the level of the lower clouds and the wind that moves the upper clouds. These three winds will more often than not be blowing in different directions, even if the differences are slight. This means that clouds at different levels will appear to move in two different directions. The upper wind cannot be felt directly, but its effect can sometimes be read as wave patterns in the highest clouds. These are not the clouds that are normally thought of as "weather" clouds; they are much higher than rain clouds, for example. If you look up into the region where aircraft contrails appear, you may see the icy upper clouds, such as the wispy cirrus. The upper winds are usually consistent with the prevailing wind direction and more dependable over long periods than the lower winds. In the northern hemisphere, the upper winds tend to snake from west to east.

The lower clouds are generally fluffy cumulus and blankets of stratus. Sometimes they are so low that they envelop us as mist or fog, the latter simply being extremely dense mist. The next time you find yourself in a mist, try looking vertically upward. It is surprising how often it is possible to see up through it, sometimes even to a blue sky, or to higher clouds that might be helpful for finding direction. This characteristic of mist is something that can confuse pilots. The runway appears clearly below an aircraft, but a few minutes later, after the pilot has turned to line up for landing, it has disappeared again even though the level of visibility has not changed. Visibility in mist and fog is all about angles; a thin blanket becomes a dense fog if you have to look horizontally through it.

More typically, the lower clouds are about 1,000 feet to a couple miles up in the atmosphere. They will move at a slightly different angle to the direction of the wind that can be felt on the ground, which can be disorienting. Both the surface wind and the wind moving these lower clouds is coming from the same source, but friction causes the wind to shift in direction as it touches the Earth's surface. In the northern hemisphere it "backs," meaning its direction shifts counterclockwise. Seen from above, the wind would appear to skid to the left as it comes into contact with the ground that slows it, because the wind is circling the center of a low pressure system, and as the wind slows it is pulled more directly in toward this center. It is important to be aware that the angle of difference between the surface wind and the "weather" wind will be influenced by your location. Over water, where the wind meets no large obstacles and so the friction is less, it might be as little as 15 degrees, but over land it can be 30 degrees or more. Being aware of this can make the difference between a feeling of comfort and awkwardness as you feel the breeze on your face consistently disagree with the direction the clouds are moving.

The clouds can help navigators on both land and sea to find their way when they loiter above islands and mountaintops, signaling land from beyond the horizon. "May the peaks of Havaiki be banked in clouds!", runs one *fangu* or chant from the people of the Tuamoto Islands in French Polynesia.

Even if the cloud is not standing over anything of importance it can still be used as a temporary guide. Marvin Creamer corrected his course following a shift in the wind by noticing that a "particularly long and heavy bar cloud appeared to shift from the port to the starboard side." Amundsen had used a similar method on his way to the South Pole:

> It was my turn as forerunner, and I pushed on. There was no longer any difficulty in holding one's course; I had the grandest cloud formations to steer by, and everything now went like a machine.

Northern pioneers like the Vikings had to endure cold voyages and long periods of overcast skies, but the clouds also brought abundant fresh rainwater, something the sailors of hotter climates like the Mediterranean often longed for. In temperate climates more journeys are taken in summer, to avoid rain, but in the hot deserts of the world people stop moving long distances and even curtail socializing in the months when the sun dominates and the clouds are scarce. In the parched Kalahari Desert, rain is treated as something magical and is addressed reverently: "If you fall on an ugly woman, you will make even her beautiful!"

Clouds never exist in total isolation, since they are the visible meeting point of hidden factors in the atmosphere, like temperature, humidity, and wind. There is no more fitting place to consider this idea than in one of the spiritual homes of holistic thought—California. There, the sun over the sea heats the water and the warm saturated air blows in off the Pacific, forming thick fogs. These low clouds hug the land and then share their water with the coastal redwood trees. The water that drips down from the giant redwoods in turn helps sustain life on the forest floor below. The intimate relationship between earth and sky that can be seen in the clouds is brought full circle by the redwoods, which grow to great heights and live for as long as 1,500 years.

CHAPTER 7

Creatures of Habit

W e are the only members of the animal kingdom to have shown any interest in navigational instruments and yet other animal species seem to find their way around impressively. Their remarkable journeys can inspire us, and they might even challenge our understanding of what we are capable of as a species.

When bees return to the hive, the other bees are able to tell from the pollen on their bodies which flowers they have visited. Bees are of course motivated by hunger and a need for energy, motivation that also drove the first human voyages of discovery. Beyond early mass migration to escape famine, it is easy to envisage an adventurous trader returning from an expedition with a shiny lump of something never previously encountered in a particular society. This prized and tradable asset would then inspire more ambitious journeys. It was trade of this sort that established contact between northern Europe and the Mediterranean in classical times. It was the desire and need for salt and precious metals that probably provided the incentive for some of the earliest sea journeys.

Male moths are known to travel vast distances in pursuit of females. Some birds travel thousands of miles to breed. Sex can be seen in the animal kingdom as a powerful motive for movement, overcoming the most imposing of natural barriers. We have seen this, too, in the human animal. In the eighteenth century, explorers returned from the Pacific with extravagant tattoos and tales of a more liberated sexual culture in places like Tahiti. Tattoos quickly embedded themselves in naval custom, and recruitment for voyages to the Pacific blossomed. Fletcher Christian's mutiny on the *Bounty* and subsequent flight to set up a new colony on Pitcairn Island is a story about naval discipline on the surface and sex, and probably love, at every layer below that.

Migration represents the greatest of feats within the animal kingdom, but homing instincts are a powerful influence, too. Coming home has always been an important part of the journey for animals and humans alike. Some journeys defy explanation. In an experiment designed to test the homing instinct, a Manx shearwater bird was flown in an aircraft from its home on the island of Skokholm off the Pembrokeshire Coast in Wales to Boston, Massachusetts. It found its way back home in twelve and a half days, covering a distance of 3,400 miles, which is not only very fast but also suggests that it was very confident of the direction in which it needed to travel. Even when it is difficult to fully explain the abilities of animals they can act as an inspiration for what is possible.

Many people can tell tales of animal feats that are intriguing and/or baffling. When I was a child my favorite pet, a miniature schnauzer dog called Muffles, jumped out of our car on the Isle of Wight. She was a small, scruffy gray dog, intelligent, but with poor eyesight and a terrible sense of smell—she could barely find a chocolate a yard from her nose. After three days of frantic searching, we started to fear the worst. The following day she turned up outside the house of my sister's friend, a house she had never been to before, three miles from where we had lost her.

Animals can help us in two distinctly different ways. We can observe their behavior and make deductions from what we see, but we can also study their methods and try to emulate them.

No animal is entirely independent of the others that share its habitat, and whether we recognize it or not we are influenced by the behavior of each other. It is worth monitoring the chain of animal reactions when moving across remote areas. Some animals are notoriously fast at reacting and the slightly slower animals use them as a cue—mammals such as deer and rabbits will take flight shortly after birds have taken to the air. This ripple effect is one of the defining features of temperate wilderness. People using animals to read human behavior is one of the oldest tricks in human conflict, as Jim Hawkins in *Treasure Island* shows us:

> All at once there began to go a sort of bustle among the
> bulrushes; a wild duck flew up with a quack, another
> followed, and soon over the whole surface of the marsh a
> great cloud of birds hung screaming and circling in the air. I
> judged at once that some of my shipmates must be drawing
> near along the borders of the fen . . . This put me in great
> fear, and I crawled under cover of the nearest live-oak, and
> squatted there, hearkening, as silent as a mouse.

The people of the Kalahari Desert use birds to indicate the presence of snakes, but also to find water.

During the eighteenth century, the Swiss naturalist Charles Bonnet brought some ants into his home and watched them scurrying to and from some sugar he had placed at one end of a table. Determined to work out how they were finding their way so efficiently, he started to tinker with their environment. He ruled out light as a clue and then ran his finger across their trail. Temporary bedlam ensued, and he was able to deduce that they were sensitive to the chemicals on the surface of the table and therefore that they were smelling their way along a scent trail left by others. The ants remind us to keep our senses tuned.

Many of the navigational techniques used by animals are familiar to us already. Caribou and wildebeest follow natural lines including rivers, valleys, lakes and ridges, while lemmings aim for mountains when crossing frozen lakes. Gannets have been removed from their home areas, released, and then observed from an aircraft. They appear to explore the local area, searching for landmarks, before successfully heading for home. Released pigeons appear to avoid flying over water and to follow landmarks in navigating their way home.

Parrot fish, sand fleas, birds, beetles, and bees, among many other species of animal, use the sun to orient themselves. Some experiments have suggested that birds have an internal sun compass accurate to within 5 degrees. Bees are one of the most intriguing solar navigators because they not only use the sun, but they then communicate direction relative to the sun to other bees with their trademark waggle dances. They are able to indicate the source of food relative to the bearing of the sun, the simplest examples being a vertical upward movement meaning "head toward the sun" and a downward movement meaning "head away from the sun." But their dance messages are intricate and sophisticated enough to cover the angles in between. The idea that one bee can "explain" to another bee how to find something naturally and more effectively than we might be able to is extraordinary.

It seems that humans do not have a monopoly on the shadow stick method, since experiments with birds have suggested they use shadows to navigate. The stick in the case of pigeons might be a sixty-five-foot-tall tree, meaning that the angular change of a shadow over a short period witnessed by a pigeon could be six times greater than seen by watching the sun itself. Shadows magnify the effect of the sun's arc for pigeons just as they do for us.

Even the most impressive of animal navigators would struggle to use the sun at night, but animal journeys do not stop at sunset. Birds such as chickadees and warblers have confidently found direction in a planetarium, and mallards and teals have also shown the ability to recognize the stars in order to navigate. The underwing moth not only orients itself using the stars but also appears to focus its efforts on the celestial equator.

The moon is such an important feature in the night sky that it would be surprising if evidence could not be found for its use by animals. Early theories of the role it played were a little off the mark. In medieval times, before migration was well understood, the Bishop of Hereford explained the seasonal disappearance of swallows at the end of the summer by saying that they flew to the moon. More recently it has been shown that dung beetles use the polarized nature of moonlight to find their way and sandhoppers altered their heading when a mirror was used to change the moonlight's direction.

The bond between animals and celestial objects appears broad and strong. Underpinning this relationship in all cases is an understanding of time: Some animals have an internal clock that is accurate to within five minutes over the course of a day. Sometimes the moon acts as the animal's timekeeper: The reproductive cycle of the Samoan palolo worm is aligned to the final quarter of the moon's phases in October and November.

Even with our understanding of celestial cues, questions about how animals navigate keep surfacing. Birds are known to take wind direction into account before setting off on long journeys, but still take off when it is overcast and even foggy. Why? Can they navigate without the help of the sun and other visual clues? Snails can find their way over relatively huge distances, a thousand feet or more, but lose this ability if they are shaken in a bag, which raises two questions: Why do they lose this ability and why were they shaken in a bag?

Vikings sailing from Norway to Greenland relied partly upon sighting the Shetland Islands. It was also necessary for skippers to stay well south of Iceland without losing contact with the landmass altogether. They did this by remaining in sight of the preponderance of marine life, including sea birds and whales, that populated the krill-rich continental shelf. The shallowness of the shelf and its proximity to land make it a perfect environment for a whole range of animals from the minute to the mighty. This telltale richness of life has assisted sailors for centuries.

Some creatures, like porpoises, favor deeper water. Canadian-American seaman Joshua Slocum, the first person to sail alone around the world, used the company of porpoises as a way of ensuring that he was not closer to land than he wanted to be. They are indeed a godsend for solo mariners, as they are happy to offer company when few other animals are. They seem to sense loneliness and appear at the right moment.

General observations about particular species are common throughout accounts of nautical voyages. Sometimes their use is straightforward: Mariners come to know that certain birds roost on certain rocks and others realize that if you pass through an animal's territory you are likely to see it, this after all is the business of a safari guide. But sometimes the use of individual animals approaches the sublime.

The Pacific Islanders took the concept to a new level with their method of *pookof*. There is an excellent account of this by the writer Stephen Thomas, who spent time living on the small Micronesian island of Satawal and studying there under the master natural navigator Mau Piailug. Mau navigated between the islands using the stars, the wind, and other navigational methods, but he also relied upon his knowledge of individual animals and where they could usually be seen. They were identified not just by their species, but by individual marks and the behavior of anything from a small bird to between ten and twenty killer whales. Some were described in general terms, others more specifically: a ray with a red spot behind its eyes, a frigate bird that climbs high in the sky, and a tan shark that makes lazy movements in the water. This method was testified to by others on the islands and is clearly not the eccentric ways of a single navigator.

The Birds

The ability of birds to reveal the proximity of land from sea has been known to sailors for thousands of years, but their greater influence on human journeys was probably in hinting at the existence of new land even longer ago. Here it is the annual rather than daily patterns that are of interest. Wave after wave of one species of bird heading out over the horizon with a seasonal regularity and dependability probably inspired and guided some of the earliest exploration and emigration.

A friendly finger of suspicion is pointed at bird migrations in two very different parts of the world. In the Pacific there are some examples that stand out, like the migratory routes of the golden plover and rare bristle-thighed curlews between Tahiti and Hawaii. It is interesting to note that the route used by the Maori fleet that sailed from Tahiti to New Zealand sometime in the fourteenth century and settled there is the same as that taken by the long-tailed cuckoo each September.

It is also known that the Irish Culdee monks of the sixth century made regular journeys between Ireland and Iceland. How they first found out about Iceland is not known for certain, although they may have read about it in the works of Pliny the Elder, Solinus, and Martianus Capella. But their journeys also passed under the migratory routes of brant geese. Skein after skein of these birds marked paths in the sky out over the horizon from their homes in places like the Shannon Estuary. Their annual exodus must have acted as a strong indicator that there was something in that direction, and it is also highly likely that their flight paths acted as navigational pointers during the monks' voyages. In many ways the monks would have been ideal candidates for this type of pioneering voyage. If the geese were suggesting foreign lands, then the monks might well have felt a duty to spread the Word of God in that direction. Their vocation was suitable for another reason: Bobbing about in the cold North Atlantic in a small boat, beneath overcast skies, waiting for a flock of geese to appear over the horizon and point the way would have been an extreme test of patience and faith.

The direction and path of bird migration can continue to enrich contemporary voyages, but the modern traveler can also find inspiration from the birds in a different form. It is one the Polynesians and monks would have appreciated, that of endurance. The Arctic tern is notorious for its seasonal sexual efforts (and puts human couples mating on romantic getaways to shame), by breeding in the Arctic and then traveling 12,000 miles from the Arctic to the Antarctic and back each year. The main benefit of this extreme migration to the tern and other avian long-haulers is the extra daylight for breeding and feeding. Some birds spend excruciating amounts of time feeding their young: One wren is reported to have fed its young 1,117 times in a single day. Long journeys for a few extra hours of daylight each day to tend to the young is essential for many birds, although this is not a concept that would be welcomed by many mothers I know.

The migratory endeavors of Arctic birds make them a logical choice for a deeper look into how birds find their way. High latitudes pose extreme challenges in terms of daylight hours, longitudinal changes, and fluctuations in the Earth's magnetic field. Extremes often help with the process of elimination, and recent research is starting to unravel some of the secrets of avian navigation. One theory is that birds can navigate using infra-sound, which is very low frequency sound, far below anything humans can hear.

There has also long been a suspicion that birds had an inner compass, an ability to navigate by magnetism. Physical evidence supporting this has been provided by the discovery of the mag-netically sensitive compound iron oxide in the brains of some species of bird. Birds are believed to be sensitive to the magnetic field's axial direction, strength, and dip (the field's angle relative to the horizontal), but not its polarity. This would mean that they can tell which way a magnetic pole is, how strong the field is, and its angle relative to the surface of the Earth, but not which pole it is—north or south. Being able to read subtle fluctuations in strength and dip may be vital not just for orientation but also for determining their location. The dip angle varies with latitude, and this may be critical. Knowing the bearing of a destination at the start of a journey is not always sufficient, since birds can become displaced by strong winds at any point along the way, and they would need to recognize this and correct for it. It is possible that the birds are using the magnetic field for both finding direc-tion and position.

Observing bird migration can point the way, but what about emulating this magnetic ability of theirs? That is easy; all that is needed is a compass, a lodestone, or even a magnetized needle suspended on a string. Ah, but those are instruments and there-fore off-limits to the natural navigator. Or perhaps it is not quite so simple.

Dr. Robin Baker conducted an experiment at Barnard Castle in the north of England in 1979 that might not have been taken seriously were he not also a member of the zoology faculty at the nearby Manchester University. The experiment involved driving blindfolded student volunteers to unknown destinations. Some had magnets attached to their heads, others did not. At their destination, the blindfolds were removed, and they were asked to orient themselves. Those who had been wrapped in magnets fared significantly worse than those who hadn't been, and the results convinced Baker of a human magnetic sense of direction that had been thrown off by the presence of the magnets.

One possible explanation for this is that if iron oxide is the key to avian magnetic navigation, then its presence might also explain the navigational ability of other animals. This compound has been found in animals including bees, flies, bacteria, homing pigeons, dolphins, and, yes, iron oxide has been found in the sinuses of human beings.

Whether or not we humans have a magnetic sense of direction, magnetic fields are known to affect rabbits, mice, and rats and influence the heart rate and function of monkeys. There is even anecdotal evidence to suggest that magnetic storms have some bearing on psychiatric conditions in humans and even possibly raise the incidence of suicides. An interesting picture of the relationship between all animals, including humans, and magnetism is building, but it is very far from complete.

Radar tracking has led researchers to discover something quite impressive about the routes birds follow. Birds in the Arctic use the sun to find direction, but not in the way that a navigator with a compass would. Instead, they use it to follow a great circle, the shortest route between two points over a sphere. Calculating a great circle is a complex process rarely undertaken by humans these days without the aid of a computer. But researchers now think that birds might achieve this, simply using one problem as an elegant solution to another one. Their imperfect tracking of time as they fly on any course with an east–west component leads them to follow the sun as its bearing changes. This curve approximates a great circle, which in turn saves them hours of flying. It may be genius on the part of the birds, natural selection, or Mother Nature. Or it may just be a lovely coincidence.

Birds can help us to understand direction even when they are not flying, since they like to congregate in sheltered spots and are habitual. Sheltered spots are usually out of the prevailing wind, which should get the deductive juices flowing. Some domestic birds have moved, but not under their own steam, surprising the scientists who analyze their DNA. The debate about contact between the South American continent and the Pacific Islands has been raging since Thor Heyerdahl's emphatic demonstration at least as to feasibility ratcheted things up a notch in 1947. Chickens in Chile have been found with DNA that can only have come from Polynesia, providing strong evidence in support of some ancient contact. Birds resting in the lee of a prevailing wind can shape a journey today, while those that died a long time ago are helping to shape our understanding of the journeys of which our ancestors were capable.

One of the things that makes it difficult for us to fully understand avian navigation demonstrates one of its greatest strengths. Navigating birds display an impressive adaptability. It does not seem to matter whether the sun or stars are visible, the terrain or magnetic field recognizable, or the wind consistent—most birds will be able to use what clues are available to find a way to complete their journey. This is perhaps the best lesson for human navigators who attempt to emulate their feats: Do not get too hooked on any one method because there will always be times when it is not there for you.

Insects

Spiders may not navigate using the wind, but they can give an indirect clue to wind direction in the orientation of their webs. Spinning a web is hard work, and it cannot have taken long for the species to "learn" that a lot of effort can be saved by not spinning against the prevailing wind. The lee of buildings and trees are favorite spots. (It is occasionally possible for a finely tuned natural navigator to combine knowledge of animal behavior with an awareness of the elements to help find direction: Arctic walruses move closer to land when a northerly wind prevails.)

The harvester termite forages by both day and night and finds its way by both sight and by "smelling" pheromones. If light levels are low, then it switches to sniffing its way to food. Logically, it seems more likely to use its sense of smell when heading toward food than away. Perhaps this reflects our own experiences. The slightest whiff of roasted cumin may draw us to the Indian restaurant, but we have a much-diminished interest in such scents as we carry our bloated bellies away.

I've already mentioned how bees navigate with regard to the sun. They also demonstrate the importance of a nondirectional aspect of wayfaring. Their dance not only indicates the direction of food but also the distance to it. They manage to convey this by waggling their abdomen from side to side: the more wags the greater the distance. Experiments have shown that this distance is not a true "over the ground" distance, but a measure of how far the bee will have to fly through the air. In still air conditions the two things are the same, but if there is a headwind, then this will be conveyed as a greater "distance." This is something we experience regularly: We tend to overestimate the distance walked when traveling uphill, into a headwind, or over difficult terrain.

The bees' understanding of the sun's arc is an inspiration. Bees manage not only to navigate using the sun and to communicate this direction to their comrades but also to extrapolate where the sun will be from one observation to the next journey. They do not predict the sun's movement perfectly, but are finely enough tuned to it to understand that if their destination was in the direction of the sun twenty minutes ago it may be several degrees to one side of it now. If they are deprived of a sight of the sun for a period of hours they can still find their way using the sun, even though it will be in a different part of the sky.

Since a full understanding of the way animals navigate is beyond even the scientific community, the most rewarding approach for the navigator is to take inspiration from the ingenuity and diversity of the methods that the animals use. This broad range can be found from the cold world of the Inuit, who instinctively read the behavior of their sled dogs, to the heat of the desert and the pigeons that have saved lives in the search for water.

The full list of navigational clues that the animals can offer would be a very long one, but two broad lessons can be drawn from observing them. The first is that we are still part of the animal kingdom and therefore probably capable of a lot more than we suspect.

The second regards approach. Birds and many other animals have learned the benefits of a range of complementary navigational methods. They have discovered, through natural selection, that navigation can be a life or death issue and that relying too heavily on one method is going to lead to problems at some point. This overlapping approach is a good one for human navigators to emulate, not just to preserve life, but also because it is an excellent way of enriching it.

CHAPTER 8

Where Am I?

Navigation is not just about working out which way you need to go, it is also about understanding where you are. Our position in the world and the universe is relative, something that has been known for a long time, but acutely well since Einstein. There is no absolute way of explaining where you are in the world, only systems and conventions for explaining where you are relative to one or two other points. If someone calls your cell phone and asks where you are, you might reply "New York City" if the person is in another part of the United States, "Central Park" if they are in New York, but not with you, or "At the Bethesda Fountain," if they are in the park but have not found you. These are all labels that help someone else frame where you are relative to them. They may or may not be helpful, but they would be meaningless to someone who did not know these naming conventions.

What if you are somewhere with no landmarks? Latitude and longitude is the modern convention that is used to explain where we are relative to the fixed line halfway between the poles, the equator, and the one fixed artificial line of the Greenwich

Meridian, which runs from the North Pole to the South Pole through Greenwich. The poles and the equator would exist as relative points and a line whether humans had existed or not. There is a huge difference in natural terms between north/south and east/west. Even without a convention for describing latitude, if you head north for long enough you will eventually reach a point that is as far north as you can go, the pole: If you carry on any farther in any direction you will be heading south. In the words of the polar explorer Robert Peary, you have found yourself at "the point where north and south and east and west blend into one."

If you head east or west from any latitude other than the poles, you can carry on going east or west forever, coming back to your starting point and carrying on east or west, over and over again. This is because east is the direction that the sun rises on average, and wherever you are in the world the sun will always appear to rise east of you. East and west did not have any geographical reference lines until we invented them; there are no natural ones. In 1884 the International Meridian Conference took place in Washington, D.C., to decide which of the many recognized meridian lines (through Washington D.C., the Great Pyramid at Giza, Jerusalem, and Copenhagen to name but a few) would become the accepted principal international line of reference. Due to its established international popularity, Greenwich was chosen as the line to mark 0 degrees longitude for all nations. The French resisted this choice and on some contemporary charts, reference to the Paris Meridian can still be found today.

The Meridian Conference reflected the fact that latitude is a reference to natural difference and longitude is only an arbitrary one. The sun and stars behave with clearly observable difference as you head north or south, but they appear in exactly the same place when you head east or west. They do of course rise and set at different times depending on your longitude, which gives us jet lag and the only meaningful astronomical difference. This is why navigators have always found estimating latitude a fairly straightforward business, while estimating longitude was a great problem until the eighteenth century.

Dead Reckoning

On August 2, 1947, a civilian airliner called *Star Dust* took off from Buenos Aires and flew west toward Santiago, Chile. There was an important diplomat and a suspected Nazi sympathizer among the six passengers. The radio operator reported being minutes from Santiago just before the aircraft disappeared without trace. It was not found for fifty years, prompting many conspiracy theories, including the involvement of a UFO.

The wreckage emerged from a thawing glacier in 1998. *Star Dust* had crashed because the navigator was using the recognized method for navigating in remote areas and had assumed that by flying at a particular speed through the air in a certain direction, the aircraft must be in a certain position. His calculations led him to believe they had cleared the Andes Mountains and were close to their destination. The clouds meant that they had no way of telling where they were visually and so they relied on these basic mathematical calculations.

In fact they had flown into the high very fast winds of the jet stream—the narrow air currents in the Earth's atmosphere—

which, unfortunately for them, were headwinds. They descended toward what they thought was Santiago, only to crash into the mountains many miles east of where they thought they were. It was not the fault of the navigator or the crew, because the jet stream was a phenomenon that wasn't yet well understood. They had lost their lives to the limitations of a navigation method known, in this case rather too appropriately, as "dead reckoning."

Dead reckoning is very straightforward, in theory. If you know which way you have been heading, how long you have been traveling, and the speed you have been moving, then a simple calculation should reveal where you are relative to your starting point. In its most basic form it works like this: If you walk north from a hotel at 4 mph for one hour, then you must be four miles north of your hotel. You have worked out where you are, even if you do not recognize the area at all.

At sea, the lack of easy reference points meant that knowledge of position was treasured. Landmarks were valuable for coastal sailing, but once out of sight of land, the earliest sailors had only three pieces of knowledge at their ready disposal. They could work out the rough direction they had sailed, they could make a rough estimate of how long they had been at sea and therefore how far they had traveled, and, most critically, they knew where they had come from. This last point is often overlooked today: The ease with which we can summon our exact position at any time has devalued the previously sanctified knowledge of where we were at an earlier moment.

Alexander the Great understood the importance of knowing where you had come from in order to calculate where you were. He did not have any navigational equipment, but he was not short of manpower. He used designated soldiers or *bematists* (from the Greek word *Bema*, or single pace), poor souls whose responsibility it was to count the number of steps the army had marched in a day. It is a technique still taught, but not much used, in the military today.

We do pay our respects to dead reckoning in a casual way in some modern journeys. A long-haul flight of perhaps nine hours might be viewed in this rough way. If asked by a child how far it is to go, a glance at the watch might reveal that six hours have passed and we are approximately two-thirds of the way to the destination—without entering the cockpit or glancing at a GPS, chart, or compass.

Dead reckoning became the difference between life and death at sea for thousands of years. The origin of the term is not known for certain, but it is popularly believed to be derived from "deduced reckoning." Another theory is that it might stem from dead-water reckoning, because the earliest forms of nautical dead reckoning did not take currents or tides into account. Dead reckoning is still taught to land, air, and sea navigators, although its use as the primary means of navigation is waning. For natural navigators it is still an important method, even if it is employed for general interest rather than accuracy of position.

Hellish Longitude

In October 1707 the body of the English Admiral Sir Cloudesley Shovell was washed up on the shores of St. Mary's Island in the Scilly Isles. A large emerald ring was missing from one of his fingers, and some suspect that he was alive when found, smothered to death for the ring and left for others to find. Whether drowned or murdered, Shovell met his maker at the same time as 1,313 others who had sailed aboard the three navy ships, the *Romney*, *Eagle*, and the flagship, *Association*. All three ships struck the Scilly rocks and went down in minutes. The main cause: uncertainty over position. To be more accurate it was almost certainly caused by confidence in being somewhere they were not. As the old saying goes, "It is far better to be lost and know it, than to confidently believe you are somewhere that you are not."

This tragic episode in Britain's naval history, like so many tragedies, probably saved lives over time. It galvanized the nation into action in the search for a better way to fix position at sea. The huge missing piece of the jigsaw had always been longitude. The sun and stars look identical if you are sixty miles east or west of where you think you are; the only thing that changes is the time that they rise and set. This is why longitude and time are often described as being two sides of the same coin. If the sun rises one hour earlier for you than it does for someone else at the same latitude, then you know you are nearer the direction of the rising sun than them: You are east of them. One hour ahead is 1/24th of the globe, which is 15 degrees. A longitude of 15 degrees East means the sun rises one hour earlier for you than it does for people who are at your same latitude, but at the longitude of Greenwich, which as the Prime Meridian is at zero longitude.

Navigators had known the relationship between time and longitude for centuries, but nobody believed that it was possible to keep accurate time at sea and so it was regarded as an impossible calculation. English clockmaker John Harrison gave most of his working life to solving this problem by inventing the marine chronometer. His efforts have been magnificently laid out in Dava Sobel's book *Longitude*. Harrison had to convince the scientific establishment, in the form of the "Board of Longitude," that the problem could be solved by keeping time at sea. The Board were initially convinced that the answer to the problem lay in the heavens.

Use of the celestial sphere had dominated navigational positioning since ancient times. Pytheas used the sun to master his impressive latitudinal expedition, but the sky had featured as early as the second century BC in relation to longitude. Hipparchus realized that although the rising and setting of objects appeared to be the same regardless of longitude, individual celestial events would have to occur at some fixed moment in the day or night, and this moment would be related to how far east or west you were on the planet. Eclipses appear at different times of the day depending on the observer's position, and Hipparchus used this to propose that lunar eclipses might be used for establishing longitude. The same famous eclipse was simultaneously observed during Alexander's victorious battle at Arbela and at Carthage. They appeared, in terms of a solar day, to have taken place approximately three hours apart, which led to the belief that the two places were 45 degrees apart (3 × 15 degrees). The actual distance is closer to 33 degrees. Eclipses, although theoretically valid as chronological reference points, are not nearly frequent enough to be a practical solution for navigators on the constant move.

John Harrison faced opposition from those who propounded a celestial solution, one based around magnetic fields and more bizarre theories, including one which involved stabbing different dogs with the same knife and then plunging that knife into the "powder of sympathy" back in London at midday. The powder of sympathy, a concoction of copper sulfate that had been dried by the sun when it was in the constellation of Leo, would cause the seafaring dog to howl in telepathic sympathy, thereby revealing the time of midday in London at sea. It did not work. John Harrison's marine chronometer did work, however, and his invention revolutionized and extended the possibility of safe long-distance sea travel.

This is probably the moment to concede that longitude is not a nut that the natural navigator can crack without instruments. If a concession is allowed in the form of a watch, then it is possible to roughly estimate longitude using a shadow stick, and then comparing this to a watch set to Greenwich Mean Time. If the watch reads 6 PM when the sun is observed to be at its highest, then you must be six hours west of Greenwich, which is the same as 90° west. Naturally assessing the moment the sun is at its highest, even using shadows, is not an accurate business. Hence the invention of the sextant.

Even the most ardent natural navigator ought to concede that the problem of longitude alone warrants the whole history of the invention of navigational instruments, while continuing to assert that the instruments are never more important than the journey itself.

Heavenly Latitude

Pytheas's method for finding latitude was quite straightforward. The ratio of the midday shadow length on the equinox to the height of the "stick" casting it could be used to calculate latitude.

The sun is the easiest object to find in the sky, but not the easiest object to use for finding latitude because of its seasonal variation in height above the horizon. It takes tables and calculations to work out your latitude using the sun on most days of the year, something the fifteenth-century astronomer Zacuto helped the Portuguese with. The stars' paths do not vary over the months: As we have seen, they rise and set in the same place each day of the year, which make them a more useful means of calculating latitude.

If your latitude changes, you will see a different part of the celestial sphere. Even if you walk only ten steps to the south and then look up, the night sky will have "shifted" from north to south a tiny and imperceptible amount. If you travel any significant distance north or south, then the half of the celestial sphere and therefore the stars you can see will have changed substantially. The key is always the celestial sphere.

If you imagine standing at the North Pole, the North Star will, as we know, be overhead and therefore 90 degrees above the horizon. If you stand at the equator, the North Star will not be visible as it will be sitting on the horizon, exactly 0 degrees above it. The latitude of the North Pole is 90 degrees, and the latitude of the equator is 0 degrees. If you stood halfway between the pole and the equator, then your latitude would be 45° north, and Polaris would appear 45 degrees above the horizon. The geometry is kind. Wherever you are in the world the celestial pole closest to you will appear the same angle above the horizon as your latitude. If you are in Sydney the empty black spot that is the south celestial pole, which you have identified using the Southern Cross, will be just under 34 degrees above the horizon because Sydney's latitude is just under 34° south.

This means that when you have identified the North Star (or south celestial pole), all you need to do is measure its angle above the horizon. To do this with accuracy requires the use of a sextant and practice, but the principle can be demonstrated very easily with no tools. The average outstretched fist is 10 degrees wide. If you are at 55° north, then Polaris will appear five-and-a-half fist-widths above the horizon. On a clear night you can now find north to within 1 degree and estimate your approximate latitude in under a minute with only your bare hands.

An extended fist can be used to roughly gauge 10 degrees.

The Arabs are known to have used the height of the North Star for latitude in the Indian Ocean, and the Vikings, like most cautious navigators of the time, knew two broad types of sailing: They would refer to the coasts or keep an eye on their latitude. The Tahitians have been aware for centuries, if not millennia, that if they crossed the equator into the southern hemisphere, then

Polaris would become invisible: "When you arrive at the Piko-o-Wakea, you will lose sight of Hokupua." It is the only method known to have been used by Columbus.

The Roman poet Lucan used the following lines in his version of the aftermath of Pompey's defeat at Pharsalus:

Is Arctophylax descending at all from the summit of the mast, and is the Cynosure brought nearer to the sea, then is the bark making towards the harbors of Syria. Then does Canopus receive us, a star content to wander in the southern sky, dreading Boreas: speed onward with it also to the left, beyond Pharos, the bark in the mid sea will touch the Syrtes.

The first line refers to the star Arcturus: Its height against the mast is shown to be a guide to latitude. Canopus, a southern star, can only "receive" a ship once the ship has traveled far enough south.

It is possible to gauge latitude from the stars in more ways than one. At the North Pole, Orion and the stars on the celestial equator will skim along the horizon, moving parallel to it. As we have seen, at the equator no stars graze the northern or southern horizons, but in midlatitudes, stars circle around the celestial poles, and some of them will touch the horizon as they do so. As they turn counterclockwise around the North Star, the stars that graze the horizon will depend on your latitude. In other words, the radius of this circle is the same as the observer's latitude, and so the farther north you travel the larger this circle becomes. This was something that Pytheas realized, and when he wrote, "the Summer Solstice was the Arctic Circle," what he meant was that radius of the circumpolar stars was 66 degrees, and he knew that he must have been at the same latitude. By becoming familiar with the stars at the outer edge, the ones grazing the horizon at your destination, you can hold the same latitude.

Similarly, since the stars rise, set, and pass over the same points on Earth every single day of the year, once you know which stars pass above your destination you can use that star to hold the right latitude for your destination. This method will keep you on the right latitude, but not tell you anything about longitude. For example, if you keep the very bright orange star Arcturus passing overhead, then you are on the same latitude as Mumbai, but also Honolulu, Mexico City, and many other places.

The same method can be used in reverse. With practice it is possible to gauge your latitude by looking vertically above you and identifying a star that is passing overhead. If you know the declination (celestial latitude) of that star, then you know your latitude. For example, if you look up and spot the bright star Capella directly overhead, then you must be 48° north, as that is Capella's declination. Not many people know the declination of many stars, but it does not take long to look at a star chart or the Internet to learn a couple for your home and destination before a journey. It is possible to get within about 1 degree when gauging whether you are under a particular star or not, which translates to an accuracy of seventy miles. Looking to the zenith was one of the key methods used by Marvin Creamer during his circumnavigation.

Keeping Track

An intimate knowledge of the landscape can be combined with a near-instinctive mental "log" of position. This is an imprecise but effective method that has also been used in deserts, on the Pacific, and by other seafarers for thousands of years. One Saharan Tuareg explained to me how he always knows the direction of the nearest significant towns or villages. This is not a sixth sense, but a graphic way of mentally keeping track of movement. Instead of thinking in terms of number of miles traveled in a particular direction, the Tuareg focus on the direction of three villages moving relative to their position, a skill constantly honed by a need to know which way to head if things go wrong out in the desert. Since their understanding of the landscape is so good, the bearings to the villages do not need to be perfect, they only need to be good enough to bring a Tuareg within sight of a landmark they recognize.

A very similar method has been used in Micronesia, and, as with everything Pacific, it has a couple of unique twists. The anthropologist Thomas Gladwin documented the indigenous use of a mental log keeping system called *Etak*. Like the Tuareg, the Micronesian sailors would keep a mental note of the direction to each island, but they did it by imagining which star each island was under even though for the most part they could not see the island, only the star. The other twist, somehow more aesthetic than essential, is that the islanders imagined that their canoe remained stationary on the ocean and that the islands would flow past them in the opposite direction to their travel, moving under different stars with the passage of time. This is no more complex than imagining a town to be in front and to your right at the start of a walk and behind to your right at the end of a walk. It is simply a method for keeping a mental picture of where you are relative to your important surroundings.

The natural observer and traveler may choose not to view the world in terms of longitude and latitude or relative bearings at all. Instead, they may opt for general knowledge and general clues. At its most facetious this way will help a lost traveler deduce that if they are surrounded by ice or sand dunes, they are not standing at Hollywood and Vine. On a fairly useless but entertaining level, it may help a gastronome to gauge which part of Europe or India they are in from the diet and taste of the food. The ancients held much more stock in this general approach than modern geography can support. The philosopher Posidonius believed that the different bands of the earth, the varying latitudes, had not only similar climates due to the angle of the sun, but that the people in each would be found to be of very similar mental and physical character.

Aside from crazy culinary methods and ancient philosophy there are some more genuine and practical ways of deducing your location, but even these require attuning the senses and a bit of lateral thinking.

Animals can be used, as we have seen. One navigator noted that the 30,000 pairs of gannets nesting off Grasholm are used by experienced locals "as an indicator of the presence of Pembrokeshire almost without thinking about it." Knowledge of the behavior of animals can help pinpoint location in a general or specific sense. Humpback whales migrate from Hawaii to Alaska each year, and there is one place off the coast of Alaska where they hunt in teams, an incredible display that is not known to occur anywhere else on Earth.

The same theory can be applied to plants, including trees. There are a lot more palm trees on the Hawaiian islands than the coast of Maine. Each species of plant and animal has its own idiosyncrasies. Each flower has its own preferred environment and will thrive if it finds it. It is sometimes possible to find patches of woodland that support explosive bluebell populations, and this can help to build a picture, a sort of bluebell map, of an area of woodland each spring.

Our sense of sight likes to bully the others from our thoughts, but it is never the only one available to us. Legend has it that in the 1820s a blind Polynesian navigator called Kaho and his son Po'oi helped navigate a flotilla of lost canoes back to Tonga. One of the methods Kaho used was to dip his hand into the sea and taste the spray. He was likely judging waves and swell as well as getting information about the stars from his son, but one of his descendants has claimed that he was also assessing the temperature of the water. Kaho was supposedly able to tell which sea zone, or *fanakenga*, they were in solely by feeling the water. This may just about be plausible since the range in temperature in that region is about 4°C across the sea zones.

As these few examples highlight, there is no limit to the interest that can be taken in this area, serious or otherwise, and the help that it can give in understanding where you are, in every sense. The possibilities are only limited by our own curiosity. "Where am I?" is one of those questions that can be answered with a latitude and longitude, "In a Kasbah in the High Atlas," or a hundred lines that take in the sun, stars, moon, planets, vegetation, animals, descriptions of the water and air and even the taste of the tagine.

It is time to leave this brief look at the broader prompts by considering a couple of clues for sailors. Marvin Creamer wrote of his plans of establishing his position as he closed on the African coast: "In making our approach we would be able to tell whether we were north or south of Dakar by noting the type of vegetation—desert or steppe—on the shore."

My own experiences in this area are less scientific than even that broad brushstroke. At the end of each year, as the hurricane season passes, there is a gathering of sailors in the Canary Islands, preparing to set out across the transatlantic route to the Caribbean. There are always lighthearted and friendly discussions taking place among kindred spirits down at the water's edge. There is usually plenty of sound advice to be had for free, mixed in with good gallows humor and exaggerations. I remember very clearly my first chat about the best route to take with a skipper who had done it a couple of times before. She offered me an age-old method for establishing my latitude. "Head south until the butter melts," she said, "and then turn right."

Unity: An Epilogue

Is the light vanished from our golden sun,
Or is this daedal-fashioned earth less fair,
That we are nature's heritors, and one
With every pulse of life that beats the air?
Rather new suns across the sky shall pass,
New splendour come unto the flower, new glory to
    the grass.
And we two lovers shall not sit afar,
Critics of nature, but the joyous sea
Shall be our raiment, and the bearded star
Shoot arrows at our pleasure! We shall be
Part of the mighty universal whole,
And through all Aeons mix and mingle with the
    Kosmic Soul!

          —From *Panthea* by Oscar Wilde

I n the beech wood near where I live I came across a large,
dominant tree that had dissuaded all other trees from
attempting to grow too close to it. The ground around it was
a thick carpet of undergrowth and ivy. On one side of this great
beech the light and dark green ground was flecked with white.

The branches on one side of the tree had been favored by the birds and they had chosen to demonstrate this by shaking their tails and flicking their paintbrushes at the ground below it.

It would have been too easy to overlook those white splatterings; I must have done it a hundred times before. But on that occasion my senses were alert enough to catch them. The observation led to thought and after a short pause in the shade of the tree, there followed a simple theory. There were more branches on one side of the beech tree than the other, which was why the birds had favored it. The tree's need for sunlight and the sun's southern arc suggested that the white flecks of guano were a clue to south. The sun, tree and birds had come together to form a "bird poo compass," one that would likely go unnoticed by all who do not take an interest in the strange art that is natural navigation.

In this book it has been necessary to divide the natural world up into its domains. This is the best way to get to know the different faces of natural navigation, but the joy is to be had by experiencing it in everything we encounter in the world around us. We like to compartmentalize—it is one of our many coping strategies for the complex world in which we live—but sometimes there is more fun to be had by letting the divisions crumble.

If we head out on a clear night to look up at the stars, it does no harm to sense the breeze on our faces or to reflect how the clarity of the air itself provides clues as to the relationship between sun, air, and water. The stars will not disappear if we pick up the smell of a log fire on the breeze and realize that this is being carried across from the street to the west of us, or if we hear an owl and note that he is in the woods to the south. The time we invest in trying to both fathom and observe the natural world yields a reward—an insight into the interconnectedness of nature.

There is delight to be found in esoteric connections. We can watch the long straggles of wool on sheep to confirm the wind direction, as the sheep themselves follow the shade of great oaks round the tree on a hot summer's day, like a clock and a compass.

On the shores of Chichester harbor, on the south coast of England, there is a village called Bosham; it is the type of place that lazy guidebooks refer to as sleepy and pretty. It is reputedly the spot where King Canute, tired by the unquestioning obsequiousness of his subjects, ordered back the tide to demonstrate the very visible limit of his powers. Canute was given a further tragic reminder of our impotence against nature when his young daughter was drowned in the millstream.

I can remember visiting Bosham with my wife about six years ago. We walked around the village and then looked in on the thousand-year-old church, where Canute's daughter is believed to have been buried. The village is situated in one of those meeting points of land and water where history was always going to happen; every square inch of the place has probably had its moment. The truth is that I was ignorant of almost all of it on our first visit. We walked from the church to a pub at the water's edge, bought a couple of drinks, and sat, looking out at the scene of coastal perfection. I felt very little. It was undeniably "pretty" and certainly tranquil, if not "sleepy." There was some small movement as a few kayakers waded out into the shallow water. All the ingredients had been assembled for a perfect moment, if such a thing exists, but instead I felt no more moved than if I were looking at the picture on a postcard of Bosham.

A little over a year ago my wife and I returned to Bosham. We followed a similar route—it is a small village, and there are not many to choose from. My face was picking up the subtle shifts in the breeze as we moved past a boathouse and then I strained to make sense of a strange curve in the wood of a churchyard yew, but failed.

We stood at the water's edge with our drinks, a few feet or so from where we had sat six years before, and looked out. The scene was the same, and yet it could not have been more different. The sun was dropping to the north of west, and it arranged the land and water around us. The trees reflected the years of sun and wind. The first quarter moon pointed south and then ganged up with the strong smells of marine decay to describe the neap tide. The last of the sea breeze was greeting us and telling us that there would be a change soon. My senses fought to take in all the clues, and my mind worked excitedly to fit the jigsaw together. I think my wife could sense the cogs whirring. She may have thought that I was worried about something and asked if I was enjoying myself. "Yes," I replied. And I meant it.

A few minutes later I asked her where she would like to eat. I followed her as she tracked the scent of fish and chips to the pub around the corner.

Sources and Notes

One of the aspects of natural navigation that either attracts or repels is the breadth and diversity of the subject. I have drawn from sources that range from ancient and modern texts, through my own experiences, to conversations with contemporary nomads. Although it would be impossible to list every influence on my understanding and therefore this book, I have endeavored in the following pages to outline where there are clear sources for facts, quotes, or ideas. This is easiest when the ideas are specific and the influence limited; it is harder when a work or individual has had a broader impact. There are inevitably some ideas that have been with me too long to recall where they came from and whether they are original. Also, wherever I have been forced by a need for brevity to give a subject less attention than would be ideal I have tried to point the direction for further reading.

Special acknowledgment must go to Marvin Creamer, who allowed me both access to his unpublished account of his extraordinary circumnavigation without instruments and permission to quote from it in this book.

Harold Gatty also deserves special mention, as his book, *Nature is Your Guide: How to Find Your Way on Land and Sea,* was the book that drew me further in to the subject over a decade ago and has also been a valuable source in many areas of this book, particularly Chapter 1. David Burch's book *Emergency Navigation* has furthered my understanding of many celestial and nautical phenomena and their use. David Lewis's book, *We, the Navigators,* gave me an invaluable insight into indigenous Pacific nautical methods. *The Vintage Book of Walking* has done a great job of identifying those who have anything pertinent or beautiful to say about the subject. Anthony Aveni's *People and the Sky* has been a constant reference for ancient and mythological connections with the sky. Horace Beck's *Folklore and the Sea* is a trove. Granta's *The Arctic: An Anthology* and *The Antarctic: An Anthology* have helped me track down vivid recollections from the highest latitudes. George Silberbauer's *Hunter and Habitat in the Central Kalahari Desert* explored the relationship between one society and the natural world at a level that has been helpful in many areas of my research.

Nearly all references to the Libyan Sahara are thanks to the patience of Muhammed, Amgar, and Khadiro, Tuareg friends who showed admirable patience as I gently interrogated them while we walked together through more than 90 miles of the Fezzan desert.

General Notes

Where no location is specified, a northern temperate location can be assumed.

Introduction: The Art of Natural Navigation

9 "A minimum of equipment and any available food is loaded . . ." • Lewis (1972)

10 "When I stay in one place I can hardly think at all" • I first came across this quote of Rousseau's in Minshull (2000).

11 "Aboriginal men" • Baker (1981).

12 "the legend of Nana-Ula" • Lagan (2006).

12 "a good navigator is quietly revered, a poor one gently ridiculed" • Gagne cited in MacDonald (1998).

13 "survival technique" • There are many who approach the subject from the perspective of "bushcraft," rather than "survival." Their aim is to have a good working knowledge of the outdoors and bring themselves closer to nature through practical skills that require a minimum of modern technology. Their interest is much closer to my perspective than the survival school of thought, the differences sometimes only lying in emphasis. The bushcraft approach is very practical, with much less interest in the historical, mythical, or philosophical background that I like to think of as integral to my approach to "natural navigation."

Another variant of the survival philosophy is what has been termed "emergency navigation" by David Burch in his excellent nautical book of that name. There is a lot to be said for the argument that a navigator should not come apart at the seams if all electronics or compasses are lost. This need not be the primary motive for learning these skills, however, as the journeys where all the instruments fail will never rival the number of those where they do not.

15 "the answer must be 'no'" • There is a fair argument that those who are responsible for others' safety have a duty to understand the rudiments of natural navigation so that they can perform their duties in the event of major systems failure or electromagnetic catastrophe. This applies equally in a civilian or military context.

15 "key to unlocking a fascinating text in the Earth's rich library." • My thanks to Richard Webber, who described natural navigation in this way after a private course in the South Downs.

16 "a town is in the direction of some buildings we can see" • Baker (1981).

16 "the loss of native navigational methods in North Alaska" • MacDonald (1998) citing Nelson (1969).

16 "This point was demonstrated when in 1990" • MacDonald (1998) citing Picco (1993).

21 "Captain Fanning" • Beck (1973).

22 "much more sensitive to shape than we are to color" • Gatty (1958).

23 "The clouds were at first violet, but they quickly caught the train of colors" • Cook (1900).

23 "Harold Gatty referred to the smells" • Gatty (1958).

23 "like color-blind men" • Carthy (1956).

25 "Our taste buds are most sensitive to sweet, sour, salt and bitterness" • Technically there is a fifth taste, now widely

identified as umami (sometimes called *savory*), but it does not change this relationship between smell and taste.

25 "First he looked at it, then he smelled and finally tasted it" • Beck (1973).

26 "the timbre of the echo gave clues" • Beck (1973).

26 "Ben Underwood" • CBS News. Having overcome blindness, Ben Underwood sadly lost his battle with cancer on January 19, 2009.

26 "He watched them navigate their way in kayaks" • Gatty (1958) citing Spencer F. Chapman from "On Not Getting Lost." *The Boys' Country Book.* (ed. John Moore). Collins, 1955. Pages 39–48.

27 "songlines" • For more on this, see Bruce Chatwin's *Songlines.* Vintage, 1998.

28 "A lot could be written on the delight of setting foot on rock" • Spufford (2008) quoting Scott (1913).

29 "kinesthetic" • Baker (1981).

29 "a ten minute error per twenty-four hours" • "An Experiment in Temporal Disorientation" *ACTA Psychologica* 1 (1935) Macleod and Roff.

29 "Our perception of minutes, days and months changes as we get older" • Halberg, Franz, Robert B. Sothern, Germaine Cornélissen, and Jerzy Czaplicki "Chronomics, human time estimation, and aging" *Journal of Clinical Interventions in Aging.* 3:4 (2008) • 749–760.

30 "Gwi tribe measure time in days and fractions of days" • Silberbauer (1981).

30 "We are at Number Fourteen Pony Camp" • Scott (1913).

31 "heave-to and wait for dawn" • Lewis (1972).

Chapter 1: Vale and Dune: The Land

32 "Tuareg... tend goats ..." • Personal conversations with the Tuareg in the Fezzan region of the Libyan Sahara. March 2009.

36 "Farm life for a boy ..." • Creamer (1985).

36 "an appreciation of the importance of scale" • The importance of scale always becomes apparent during the outdoor courses I run. A clue that is obvious to one person can get easily overlooked by someone else, standing next to them, who is focusing too intently on either the near or the far. A classic example is a frantic search for mosses or lichens, when miles of coastline are visible.

37 "sunlight bouncing off ..." • My thanks to Russell Cook who kept his senses tuned on holiday after attending a course in 2008. He came across a tree growing "away from the sun," but toward a mirror glass building in Majorca.

39 The habits of burrowing animals were brought to my attention by David Langmead during a course at West Dean College.

39 "Gamama was bitten by a snake" • Silberbauer (1981).

40 "drumlins" • This was flagged by Nick Veck during a course.

41 For more on John Hillaby's expedition, see Hillaby (1973).

45 "heliotropic plants" • Galen, Candace "Sun Stalkers" *Natural History* May 1999.

46 "giant cactus of Tucson" • Johnson, D. S. "The Distribution and Succession of the Flowers of the Giant Cactus in Relation to Isolation" in "The American Association for the Advancement of Science Section G, Botany" *Science* 17 December 1915, 42: 874-880

46 "wild lettuces . . ." and the other specific examples here • Gatty (1958).

47 "fiery wheel will come forth" • Thorpe (2001).

50 Leonardo da Vinci's observations • Gatty (1958).

53 "In the nineteenth century a Scottish writer, James Fergusson" • Porteous (1928) citing Fergusson (1868), *Tree and Serpent Worship: Illustrations of Mythology and Art in India in the First and Fourth Centuries after Christ.*

57 "zig zag" • I came across this reference to Stephen Graham in Minshull (2000).

57 "Tiananmen Square" • Aveni (2008).

59 "Effects of aspect on weathering: anomalous behavior of sandstone gravestones in southeast England" • Williams and Robinson (2000)

60 "the trumpet shall sound" • 1 Corinthians 15:52

61 "variegated *Scindapsus* plant" • Freeman in Bechtel and Churchman (2002).

65–66 sand dunes • For the defining work on the behavior of sand in the desert, see Bagnold (1941).

67 "flight into the Arctic Circle in 2005" • I piloted a Piper Archer from White Waltham, England, to Kiruna, Sweden, in June 2005. I was joined on this holiday by Ross Collett, who started the trip with no previous aviation experience and finished as a very capable navigator.

68 "a man carrying a lantern" • Cook (1900).

69 "Niqiq" and "Uangnaq" • MacDonald (1998).

70 "A water-sky, a land blink, or some other sign" • Cook (1900).

70 "basking walruses" • MacDonald (1998).

70 "An Inuit called Aipilik" • MacDonald (1998).

Chapter 2: The Perfect Illusion: The Sun

75 The early history of navigation referred to throughout the book is collated from many of the sources that can be found in the bibliography, but two excellent volumes for getting an overview are *The Haven-Finding Art, A History of Navigation from Odysseus to Captain Cook* by E. G. R. Taylor (1956) and *No Star at the Pole* by David and Joan Hay (1972).

75–7 Pytheas features in passing in most histories of early geography or navigation, but for more thorough coverage I can recommend Barry Cunliffe's *The Extraordinary Voyage of Pytheas the Greek* (2001).

80 "Truman Capote" • I was reading Capote's gruesome but excellent account of real-life multiple murder, *In Cold Blood*, while on a short break from researching this book. It struck me then, as it has since, that great authors stand out in their ability to observe and record the vivid natural effects that physical relationships like orbits have. I have also noticed it in the lyrics of songs, such as the "Hymn of the Big Wheel" by Massive Attack.

83 "The Shadow Stick" • I first came across shadow stick methods in outdoor and survival literature, but through experimenting and reading around the subject discovered that the survival approach usually only touches the surface. The fascination developed for me from delving deeper into areas such as ancient astronomy. I can recommend *The History and Practice of Ancient Astronomy* by James Evans (1998), *Ancient Astronomy* by Clive Ruggles (2005) and *Astronomy Before the Telescope* edited by Christopher Walker (1996).

89 "to fly solo across the Atlantic" • In May 2007 I flew solo in a Cessna Caravan from Goose Bay, Newfoundland, to Oxford, England, refueling in Narsarsuaq (Greenland), Reykjavik (Iceland), and Wick (Scotland).

94 "honing your skills" • One way to practice is to estimate the direction of the sun and then check how you did on the Internet. The U.S. Naval Observatory Web site, http://aa.usno.navy.mil/data/docs/AltAz.php, is one of many that allows you to check the azimuth (bearing) of the sun or moon from any position on Earth and at any time by plugging in your latitude and longitude and a date.

95 "It is however a more complex concept . . ." • The change in angle of the sun's arc with latitude is the reason why it is not a good idea to place too much stock in the "watch method." At certain latitudes the hands of an analog watch can be used to find direction in a rough way. The method is as follows: The watch is held horizontally and the hour hand is oriented so that it points toward the sun. From the UK, the angle that is halfway between the hour hand and 12 o'clock will point approximately south. However, this method does not take seasonal clock changes into account; it only works well at certain latitudes, and the potential for inaccuracy is great. It is more satisfying—and useful—to gain a fundamental understanding of nature that will serve you well in any part of the world.

98 "hints in Norse myth" • Karlsen (2003).

99 "sun warms the glaciers" • Gatty (1958).

Chapter 3: The Firmament

102 "squid fishermen use metal halide lamps" • Klinkenborg, Verlyn *National Geographic Magazine* November 2008.

102 "I was once asked by a Tuareg man in the Sahara" • Amgar, a Tuareg, explained that his father was "old Tuareg" and he was "new Tuareg." He regularly implied that there had been a generational shift in knowledge and customs between them and that this was the reason for his lack of understanding of the night sky.

103–4 "I have never yet seen an Indian who mounted the ladder of human progress" • Dodge (1883).

105 "constellations do not noticeably change shape" • The stars are moving and moving quickly and therefore the constellations do change shape, but not noticeably over several lifetimes, only over thousands of years.

106 "a star in the north that appears not to move" • Polaris, the North Star, is situated very close to the north celestial pole, but not exactly on it. It therefore does move, tracing a tiny circle around the pole. For those looking for pinpoint accuracy, when the star Kocab, which is in the same constellation as Polaris, Ursa Minor, is vertically above or below Polaris, then Polaris is giving an extremely accurate indication of true north. When Kocab is to the east or west of Polaris, then Polaris is close to 1 degree to the other side of true north. For example, if Kocab is to the east, then Polaris is close to 1 degree west of true north at 359 degrees.

108 "GHA is not relevant" • It is only not relevant because there is no independent way for the natural navigator to determine what it is.

117 "it is possible to invent your own methods for finding Polaris" • Polaris can be also be found using the constellations of Auriga, Cygnus and Pegasus as well as by linking individual stars like Arcturus and Alkaid or Saiph and Betelgeuse.

118 Star names • The names referred to in this chapter come from varied sources but two good places to look for ancient or mythological references are *Star Names, Their Lore and Meaning* by Richard Hinckley Allen (1963) and *People and the Sky* by Anthony Aveni (2008).

119 "The indigenous tribes of the Kalahari" • Silberbauer (1981).

120 Finding South • With a little imagination you can use the south celestial pole even when you cannot see it. If you find the constellation Gemini and draw a line from between the heads of the twins down through Procyon, one of the brightest stars in the sky, it will point toward the south celestial pole. If you know your latitude you can also estimate how far "underground" the south celestial pole is—it will be an angle down from the horizon equal to your northerly latitude—and then follow this line to that "depth," before mentally drawing a vertical line back up to the horizon. This is an approximate method and only as accurate as your estimations, which improve with practice. There are an infinite number of ways to do this type of direction finding once you know your way around the celestial sphere. An excellent reference in this area is David Burch's *Emergency Navigation* (2008). Most navigators learn a handful of techniques and then use them regularly until they become trusted friends.

121 Orion's various aliases come from Allen (1963), Lewis (1972), and Aveni (2008).

122 "His lower half contains Rigel" • *Encyclopedia Britannica 2009 Ultimate Reference Suite.*

123 "Ahutt al-Jiddi 'ald wirk" • Bailey (1974).

123 "four minutes" • It is actually closer to three minutes, fifty-seven seconds.

124 "It was known as Sothis" • Thomson (1948).

124 "to begin their second phase of school" • Silberbauer (1981).

124 "The rising and setting rhythms of the Pleiades" • Taylor (1956).

124 "geese hunting season" • Aveni (2008).

128 "However, only five planets are easily visible to the naked eye" • The planet Uranus is just visible to the naked eye in ideal conditions as a faint blue-green point.

128 "Na-holo-holo" • Kyselka (1976).

129 "peeper into pots" • Walker (1996) citing Warner, "Traditional Astronomical Knowledge in Africa," page 312.

131 "Generally we steered by Jupiter" • Cherry-Garrard (1922).

131 "Could they have been the inspiration or guide for the three wise men" • Kyselka (1976).

131 Astrology is far from alone as a method for using nature to divine the future. Anthony Aveni keeps a record of unusual methods, including "uromancy" or the study of urine. See *People and the Sky* (2008).

132 "Plato's uncle, Critias" • Thomson (1948).

132 "Colorful figures like the sixteenth-century astrologer Arcandam" • The individual behind this prediction is

unknown, as Arcandam was a pseudonym used by more than one astrologer during this period. Kyselka (1976).

133 "Think of how many more raindrops hit the front windscreen of your car than the rear window" • This perfect metaphor is from W. S. Kalss' *Stars and Planets* (1990).

134 "The aurora was always before us as we traveled east . . ." • Cherry-Garrard (1922).

134 "Richard Nelson" • I came across Richard Nelson's work in *The Arctic Sky* by John MacDonald (1998).

135 "it is possible to tell the time by looking at the stars" • There are complex methods for using the stars to give a more accurate indication of time, but the following method can give an approximate reading of Greenwich Mean Time from the UK.

Find the Big Dipper and Polaris.

Imagine a clock face with Polaris at the center. The clock has twenty-four hour marks starting at zero in the conventional 12 o' clock position and going round counterclockwise back to the same position.

Make a clock hand by picturing a line from Polaris to the "pointers" in the Big Dipper (the two stars that liquid would run off if the "saucepan" was tipped up).

On March 7 this clock will be accurate. For every day after March 7 the clock will have run fast by four minutes, and these minutes need to be subtracted. Four minutes per day adds up to two hours per month.

One example: It is September 14, and the Big Dipper is below Polaris, the hour hand is pointing vertically down. This reads 12 o'clock on the clock (midday, not 6 o'clock as it would be if the clock face had twelve numbers), but the clock has been running fast for six months and one week, which means that it is 12½ hours fast. The time is therefore approximately 11:30 PM GMT.

Chapter 4: The Fickle Moon

138 "I can sit and gaze . . ." • Nansen (1897). I first came across this quote in Kolbert (2008).

138 "girls with small breasts" • *Encyclopedia Britannica 2009 Ultimate Reference Suite.*

139 "to time the felling of the larches needed to rebuild the bridge at Naumachia" • Porteous (1928).

139 "There had been no light all day" • Cherry-Garrard (1922).

140 "the Gwi of the Kalahari" • Silberbauer (1981).

142 "The anthropologist George Silberbauer found he could use moon phases as a calendar" • Silberbauer (1981).

143 "Premature Seal Pups" • These full moon examples are from Anthony Aveni's *People and the Sky* (2008)

143 "The moon orbits the Earth" • The moon is Earth's nearest neighbor, and while it is convenient to say that it orbits the Earth, this is an oversimplification. The proximity and size of the moon mean that it exerts a sufficiently large gravitational pull on the Earth that they actually orbit each other; in fact, they both orbit around a point in the Earth known as the barycenter, about 4,700 kilometers from the center of the Earth on a line from the center of the Earth toward the moon. It is actually nearer the surface than the center of the Earth. This is the reason that there are two high and

low tides in a 24-hour period, despite there being only one moon. One tide is being caused by the moon's direct pull on the oceans, the other is caused by the Earth's acceleration toward the moon, which leaves a bulge on the opposite side. This effect on the opposite side is often described as a "centrifugal force." The oceans on either side of the world are being pulled apart, giving two high tides instead of only one in each day.

Once the reason for two tides each day is understood, this slightly complex anomaly does not have a big impact on natural navigation, and so it is best to pretend that it does not exist. It is more practical to assume that the moon does in fact follow a simple orbit around the Earth.

143 "A carved eagle bone found in a case in France" • Aveni (2008).

143 "Castle Frazer" • Walker (1996) citing Clive Ruggles' "Archaeoastronomy in Europe."

151 "There are not many people in the world familiar with its use" • One of them is David Burch, who gives a good account in his book, *Emergency Navigation* (2008).

151 "Fishing is usually best when there is a large tidal range" • Fishermen will of course be influenced by other factors, such as whether it is the weekend, what the weather is like, etc. For a thorough analysis of the relationship between the moon and tides, see *Beyond the Moon* by James Greig McCully (2006).

Chapter 5: The Sea

155 "brain capacity" • *Encyclopedia Britannica 2009 Ultimate Reference Suite.*

158 "What we demonstrated . . ." • Creamer (1985).

159 "make an estimate using an understanding of your latitude and the season" • This requires an understanding of all the principles in chapter 2, and some practice. This practice need not be for real; it can be imaginary scenarios, dates and places tested against real data from online sources or almanacs.

160 "Some Pacific Islanders are still able to steer using the sun by making these mental interpolations almost automatically" • Lewis (1972).

161 "This tradition continues in a small way to this day" • The 1983 film *The Navigators*, by Sam Low, captures the way this is done in Satawal, Micronesia.

163 "Their passion for voyaging will yet facilitate the spread of the Gospel among them" • *52nd Annual Report of the Hawaiian Historical Society* (1943). Online.

165 "the fetch was minimal" • Creamer (1985)

165 "Think of the motion of a whip" • This lovely analogy is Jack Lagan's from *The Barefoot Navigator* (2006)

166 "each crest and trough run in unbroken lines" • Burch (2008).

166 "Captain Ward, reported that a man's testicles were the best apparatus for assessing swell" • Lewis (1972) citing E. V. Ward.

171 "Juan Ponce de Leon" • *Encyclopedia Britannica 2009 Ultimate Reference Suite.*

172 "The Kuroshio Current that flows northeast in the Pacific was observed by Captain King" • *Encyclopedia Britannica 2009 Ultimate Reference Suite.*

173 "Mataki Anuta" • Lewis, Gladwin (1970) and Sir Raymond Firth (1954). "Anuta and Tikopia: Symbiotic elements in social organization" *Journal of the Polynesian Society* 63 (1954): 87–131.

173 "I cannot account for any south-going current here . . ." • Nansen (1897). I first came across this in Kolbert (2008).

174 "floating kelp or *qiqquaq*" • MacDonald (1998) quoting Piuggaattuk (1992).

174 "the Fleisher-Harris tide predicting machine" • McCully (2006).

174–5 "The Warao people of the Orinoco delta . . ." • John Pahl, personal correspondence.

175 "Prieres des Femmes" • Heath (2000). I have found no other references to this incident and have never heard the locals refer to it. There is a possibility that this is a modern myth.

174–8 For a thorough analysis of the tides see McCully (2006).

176 "King's Mirror" • Hay (1972).

178 "Herodotus noted that the Nile discolored the water" • Ibid.

179 "giving the seawater near its mouth a muddy-yellow appearance" • European Space Agency Web site. www.esa.int/esaEO/SEMZF7R01FE_index_0.html

179 "this can sometimes be seen dramatically, because a plankton bloom colors the water" • Ahel, Barlow and Mantoura (1996).

179 "giving polar waters a signature greenness" • Gatty (1958).

179 "Nobu Shirase" • Nankyokuki (1913) in Kolbert (2008).

180 "Creamer knew that the shelf is not wide off New Zealand"
• Creamer (1985)

181 "Herodotus, when commenting that the Nile was discoloring the sea" • Hay (1972).

182 "We are seeing more prions . . ." • Creamer (1985).

182 "Isolated sightings more than 80 miles" • Burch (2008).

184 "'coo-ling, coo-ling' sounds" Gladwin (1970).

185 "the shorter rays will indicate the direction of land" • Lewis
(1972).

185 "if an eyelash can be plucked easily, then land is near" •
Lewis (1972).

186 "without ceremony" • Taylor (1956).

187 "Horace Beck recounts an amusing tale" • Beck (1973).

187 "When Joe Bett's P'int you is abreast" • Horace Beck quoting from Norman Dunan's *Dr. Grenfell's Parish* (1905).

188 "The giant 'garbage patch' created by the North Pacific
Gyre" • Bradshaw, Kate "The Great Garbage Swirl" *Maui
Time Weekly* 29 January 2009. www.mauitime.com/Articles-i
-2009-01-29-68584.113117_The_great_garbage_swirl.html

189 "Underwater" • My diving experience is limited to the
PADI Advanced Open Water Diver course. The "Underwater" section relies on the following sources:

a) Personal correspondence with Charles Bennett.

b) *Underwater Navigation* by Ralph D. Erickson. PADI. 1979

c) *How to Find Your Way: A Complete Guide to Underwater
Navigation* by Jim Foley. Dacor Corporation. 1979.

190 "Polynesian Voyaging Society" • see http://pvs.kcc.hawaii
.edu.

Chapter 6: The Elements

193 "In Polynesia, the way stars twinkle has been used to forecast rain and wind" • Lewis (1972).

193 "For the first time we saw the vapor of our breath" • Creamer (1985)

196 "In this shiftless sea of ice" • Cook (1900).

197 "From Carpathus is fifty miles with Africus to Rhodes" • Taylor (1956).

197 "the cold northerly wind was called Boreas in ancient Greece" • Ibid.

198 "something to the northeast that emits a distinct smell" • Rachel Donaldson, in a conversation during an outdoor course, explained that she could tell when it was going to snow at her home because the smell of Medway power station came in from the northeast.

200 "When crossing the undulations which ran down out of the mountain" • Cherry-Garrard (1922).

201 "as in the Palouse area of Washington state in the United States" • Gatty (1958).

203 *kino kino* • Lewis (1972).

205 "When we die, the wind blows away our footprints, and that is the end of us" • I came across this quote in Minshull (2000).

207 "Gretel Erlich" • I came across this observation of Gretel Erlich's in her "Aliberti's Ride" entry in Kolbert (2008).

208 "The runway appears clearly below an aircraft" • This observation is based on personal experience of challenging conditions while attempting to land at White Waltham airfield in Berkshire.

209 "particularly long and heavy bar cloud appeared to shift from the port to the starboard side" • Creamer (1985)

209 "It was my turn as forerunner, and I pushed on ..." • Amundsen, Roald. *The South Pole.* C. Hurst & Co., 1912, reprinted 2001.

209 "if you fall on an ugly woman, you will make even her beautiful!" • Silberbauer (1981)

Chapter 7: Creatures of Habit

213 "All at once there began to go a sort of bustle ..." • Stevenson (1883)

213 "the Kalahari ... birds" • Silberbauer (1981).

214 "Caribou and wildebeest follow natural lines ... lemmings" • Baker (1981)

214 "Gannets" • *Encyclopedia Britannica 2009 Ultimate Reference Suite.*

215 "angular change of a shadow" • Galler, Schmidt-Koenig, Jacobs and Belleville (2005)

216 "animals have an internal clock" • Baker (1981)

217 *Pookof* • Thomas (1987)

218 "Golden Plover ... long-tailed cuckoo" • Gatty (1958)

218 "Pliny, Solinus, and Martianus Capella" • Taylor (1956)

219 "fed its young 1,117 times" • Carthy (1956)

220 "birds can navigate using infrasound" • Jonathan Hagstrum Frin, personal conversation.

220 "birds are using magnetic field for both finding direction and position" • Qiu (2005)

221 "human magnetic sense of direction" • Baker (1981)

221 "Iron oxide has been found in the sinuses of human beings" • Baker, Mather and Kennaugh (1983)

221 "incidences of suicide" • Baker (1981)

222 "this curve approximates a great circle" • Qiu (2005)

222 "[Birds] like to congregate in sheltered spots" • Gatty (1958)

222 "evidence in support of some ancient contact" • Borrell (2007)

223 "Arctic walruses move closer to land" • MacDonald (1998) citing Panikpakuttuk (1992).

223 "The Harvester Termite" • Leuthold, R. H., O. Bruinsma and A. Van Huis (1976).

224 "The bees' understanding of the sun's arc . . ." • Gould (1980)

Chapter 8: Where Am I?

227 "north and south and east and west blend into one" • Kolbert (2008) citing Peary (1910).

229 My thanks to a student who showed me a French chart at the end of a course at West Dean College and my apologies for forgetting your name.

230 "Sir Cloudesley Shovell" • Royal Naval Museum Web site www.royalnavalmuseum.org/info_sheets_cloudesley _shovell.htm

234 "fifteenth-century astronomer, Zacuto" • Thomson (1948)

236 "When you arrive at the Piko-o-Wakea" • Dening (1962).

236 "Is Arctophylax descending at all from the summit of the mast" • Lucan translated by Jane Wilson Joyce. *Pharsalia.* Cornell University Press, 1993

238 "bring a Tuareg within sight" • Personal conversation with the Tuareg (2009)

239 "the 30,000 pairs of gannets nesting off Grasholm" • Lagan (2006)

240 "the range in temperature is about 4 degrees Celsius" • Lewis (1972)

Bibliography

Allen, Richard Hinckley. *Star Names, Their Lore and Meaning.* Dover Publications, Inc, 1963.

Attenborough, David. *Life on Earth.* Book Club Associates. 1979.

Aveni, Anthony. *People and the Sky.* Thames and Hudson, 2008.

Bagnold, R. A. *The Physics of Blown Sand and Desert Dunes.* Dover Publications, Inc, 1941.

Bailey, Clinton. "Bedouin Star-Lore in Sinai and the Negev." *Bulletin of the School of Oriental and African Studies.* University of London. 37.3 (1974): 580–96.

Baker, Robin, R. *Human Navigation and the Sixth Sense.* Simon and Schuster, 1981.

Baker, Robin R., Janice G. Mather, and John H. Kennaugh. "Magnetic Bones in Human Sinuses." *Nature.* 301 (1983): 78–80.

Barlow R. G., M Ahel and R. F. C. Mantoura. "Effect of salinity gradients on the distribution of phytoplankton pigments in a stratified estuary." *Marine Ecology Progress Series.* 143 (November 14, 1996): 289–295.

Bechtel, Robert B. & Azra Churchman (Editors). *Handbook of Environmental Psychology.* John Wiley & Sons, 2002.

Beck, Horace. *Folklore and the Sea.* Published for the Marine Historical Association by Wesleyan University Press, 1973.

Binding, Paul. *Imagined Corners.* Headline Review, 2003.

Borrell, Brendan. "DNA reveals how chickens crossed the sea." *Nature.* 447 (7 June 2007): 620–621

Bowditch, Nathaniel. *The American Practical Navigator.* National Imagery and Mapping Agency, 2002.

Brown Jr., Tom. *The Science and Art of Tracking.* Berkley Publishing Group, 1999.

Buchan, Alastair. *Pencil, Paper and Stars: The Handbook of Traditional and Emergency Navigation.* John Wiley and Sons Ltd, 2008.

Burch, David. *Emergency Navigation.* International Marine, 2008.

Capra, Fritjof. *The Tao of Physics.* HarperCollins, 1975.

Carpenter, Rhys. *Beyond the Pillars of Hercules.* Tandem, 1966.

Carthy, J. D. *Animal Navigation.* George Allen and Unwin Ltd, 1956

Cary, M., and E. H. Warmington. *The Ancient Explorers.* Pelican, 1929.

Cherry-Gerrard, Apsley. *The Worst Journey in the World.* Pimlico, 1922.

Cline, Duane A. *Navigation in the Age of Discovery.* Montfleury, Inc, 1990.

Coggeshall, George. *An Historical Sketch of Commerce and Navigation From the Birth of Our Saviour Down to the Present Date.* Geo. P. Putnam, 1860.

Colton, Harold S. (Managing Editor). *The Tree Ring Bulletin.* April 1937. The Tree Ring Society.

Cook, Frederick. *Through the First Antarctic Night.* Doubleday & McClure Co., 1900.

Creamer, Marvin. *The Globe Star Voyage.* Unpublished, 1985.

Crowley, Tony. *The Lo-Tech Navigator.* Seafarer Books, 2004.

Cunliffe, Barry. *The Extraordinary Voyage of Pytheas the Greek.* Penguin Books, 2001.

Cunliffe, Tom. *Ocean Sailing.* Fernhurst Books, 2000.

Dening, G. M. "The Geographical Knowledge of the Polynesians and the Nature of Inter-Island Contact" *Polynesian Navigation.* Ed. Jack Golson. A. H. & A. W. Reed, 1962.

Dewey, Jennifer Owings. *Finding Your Way: The Art of Natural Navigation.* The Millbrook Press, 2001.

Dodge, Colonel Richard Irving. *33 Years Among Our Wild Indians.* Archer House, Inc., 1883 (reprinted 1959).

Evans, James. *The History and Practice of Ancient Astronomy.* Oxford University Press, 1998.

Erickson, Ralph D. *Underwater Navigation.* PADI, 1979.

Fisher, Dennis. *Latitude Hooks and Azimuth Rings.* International Marine, 1995.

Foley, Jim. *How to Find Your Way: A Complete Guide to Underwater Navigation.* Dacor Corporation, 1979.

Galler, Sidney R., Klaus Schmidt-Koenig, George J. Jacons and Richard E. Belleville (Editors). *Animal Orientation and Navigation.* University Press of the Pacific, 2005.

Gargiulo, Federico Ezequiel. *Fire Walking.* Sud Pol, 2008.

Gatty, Harold. *Nature is Your Guide: How to Find Your Way on Land and Sea.* Collins, 1958.

Gatty, Harold. *The Raft Book.* George Grady Press, 1943.

Gekakis, Nicholas. "Circadian Mechanism Role of the CLOCK Protein in the Mammalian." *Science.* 290: 1564 (1998).

Gifford, Nigel. *Expeditions and Exploration.* Macmillan, 1983.

Gladwin, Thomas. *East is a Big Bird: Navigation and Logic on Puluwat Atoll.* Harvard University Press. 1970.

Gooley, Michael. *Trans-Africa Route Report.* Trail Finders Ltd, 1975.

Gould, James. "Sun Compensation by Bees." *Science.* 207: 44301 (1980): 545–547

Goetzfridt, Nicholas J. *Indigenous Navigation and Voyaging in the Pacific: A Reference Guide.* Greenwood Press, 1992.

Graves, Robert. *The Greek Myths.* QPD, 1991.

Greenway, Keith R. *Arctic Air Navigation.* Canada Defence Research Board, 1951.

Grimble, Arthur. *A Pattern of Islands.* John Murray Ltd, 1952.

Halpern, Daniel & Dan Frank (Editors). *The Nature Reader.* The Ecco Press, 1996.

Hay, David & Joan. *No Star at the Pole.* Charles Knight & Co. Ltd, 1972.

Heath, Nick. *The Channel Islands.* Imray Laurie Norie & Wilson, 2000.

Heath, Robin. *Sun, Moon and Earth.* Wooden Books Ltd, 1999.

Heizer, Robert F., and William C. Massey. "Aboriginal Navigation off the Coasts of Upper and Baja California." *Anthropological Papers No. 39,* Bulletin 151 (1953): 285–312.

Hewson, Commander J. B. *A History of the Practice of Navigation.* Brown, Son and Ferguson Ltd, 1951.

Heyerdahl, Thor. *Early Man and the Ocean.* George Allen and Unwin Ltd, 1978.

Hilder, Brett. *Navigator in the South Seas.* Percival Marshall & Co., 1961.

Hillaby, John. *Journey to the Jade Sea.* Paladin, 1973.

Homer. *The Odyssey.* Translated by E. V. Rieu. Penguin Books Ltd, 1946.

Hourani, George F. *Arab Seafaring*. Princeton University Press, 1951.

Hutson, A. B. A. *The Navigator's Art*. Mills and Boon, 1974.

Hyde, Lewis. *The Gift*. Random House, 1983.

Johnson, Mark. *The Ultimate Desert Handbook*. McGraw-Hill, 2003.

Kals, W. S. *Stars and Planets*. Sierra Club Books, 1990.

Karlsen, Leif K. *Secrets of the Viking Navigators*. One Earth Press, 2003.

Keenan, Jeremy. *Sahara Man: Travelling with the Tuareg*. John Murray, 2001.

Kolbert, Elizabeth (Editor). *The Arctic: An Anthology*. Granta, 2008.

Kunitzsch, Paul, and Tim Smart. *A Dictionary of Modern Star Names*. Sky Publishing, 2006.

Kyselka, Will. *An Ocean in Mind*. University of Hawaii Press, 1987.

Kyselka, Will, and Ray Lanterman. *North Star to Southern Cross*. University of Hawaii Press, 1976.

Lacey, Robert, and Danny Danziger. *The Year 1000*. Little, Brown and Company, 1999.

Lagan, Jack. *The Barefoot Navigator*. Adlard Coles Nautical, 2006.

Langley, Michael. *When the Pole Star Shone*. George G. Harrap & Co. Ltd, 1972.

Langmuir, Eric. *Mountaincraft and Leadership*. Mountain Leader Training England and Mountain Leader Training Scotland, 2003.

Laundon, Jack R. *Lichens*. Shire Publications Ltd, 1986.

Lecky, Captain. *Wrinkles in Practical Navigation*. G. Phillip and Son Ltd, 1881.

Leuthold, R. H., O. Bruinsma, and A. Van Huis. "Optical and Pheromonal Orientation and Memory for Homing Distance in the Harvester Termite *Hodotermes mossambicus* (Hagen)." *Behavioral Ecology and Sociobiology*. 1:2 (1976): 127–139.

Lewis, David. *Ice Bird*. Collins, 1975.

Lewis, David. *The Voyaging Stars*. Fontana/Collins, 1978.

Lewis, David. *We, the Navigators*. University of Hawaii Press, 1972.

Lindsay, H. A. *The Bushman's Handbook*. Angus and Robertson Ltd, 1948.

Lothrop, S. K. "Aboriginal Navigation off the West Coast of South America." *Journal of the Royal Anthropological Institute of Great Britain and Ireland*. 62 (1932): 229– 256

MacDonald, John. *The Arctic Sky, Inuit Astronomy, Star Lore, and Legend*. Royal Ontario Museum/Nunavut Research Institute, 1998.

Macfarlane, Robert. *The Wild Places*. Granta Books, 2008.

McCarthy, Cormac. *The Road*. Picador, 2007.

McCully, James Greig. *Beyond the Moon.* World Scientific Publishing Co. Pte. Ltd, 2006.

Mills, Enos A. *The Adventures of a Nature Guide.* Double, Page & Co., 1923.

Minshull, Duncan (Editor). *The Vintage Book of Walking.* Vintage, 2000.

Moore, Patrick. *Stargazing: Astronomy Without a Telescope.* Aurum Press, 1985.

Morton, Jamie. *The Role of the Physical Environment in Ancient Greek Seafaring.* Brill, 2001.

Nansen, Dr. Fridtjof. *Farthest North.* Harper & Brothers, 1897.

Newman, Bob. *Wilderness Wayfinding.* Paladin Press, 1994.

Owendoff, Robert S. *Better Ways of Pathfinding.* The Telegraph Press, 1964.

Pirsig, Robert. *Zen and the Art of Motorcycle Maintenance.* Vintage, 1974.

Porteous, Alexander. *The Forest in Folklore and Mythology.* Macmillan, 1928

Pretor-Pinney, Gavin. *The Cloudspotter's Guide.* Sceptre, 2006.

Purvis, William. *Lichens.* The Natural History Museum, London, 2000

Qiu, Jane. "Ornithology: Flight of the Navigators." *Nature.* 437 (2005): 804–806

Robinson, D. A. & R. B. G. Williams. "Effects of aspect on weathering: anomalous behaviour of sandstone gravestones in southeast England." *Earth Surface Processes and Landforms.* 25:2 (2000): 135–144.

Royer, C & Scott, M. *Underwater Navigation.* International Marine Publications Systems, 1997.

Ruggles, Clive. *Ancient Astronomy, An Encyclopedia of Cosmologies and Myth.* ABC-CLIO Ltd, 2005.

Schlereth, Hewitt. *Celestial Navigation in a Nutshell.* Sheridan House, 2000.

Scott, Robert Falcon. *Scott's Last Expedition.* Smith, Elder, 1913.

Sharp, Andrew. Ancient Voyagers in the Pacific. Penguin, 1956.

Sidgwick, J. B. *Direction Finding by the Stars.* Faber and Faber, 1944.

Silberbauer, George B. *Hunter and Habitat in the Central Kalahari Desert.* Cambridge University Press, 1981.

Slessor, Tim. *First Overland.* George G. Harrap & Co. Ltd, 1957.

Sobel, Dava. *Longitude.* Walker & Co, 1996.

Spufford, Francis (Editor). *The Antarctic: An Anthology.* Granta Publications, 2008.

Staal, Julius D. W. *The New Patterns in the Sky.* The McDonald and Woodward Publishing Company, 1988.

Stevenson, Robert Louis. *Treasure Island.* Penguin Books, 2008.

Taylor, E. G. R. *The Haven-Finding Art: A History of Navigation from Odysseus to Captain Cook.* Hollis and Carter, 1956.

Thomas, Stephen, D. *The Last Navigator.* Ballantine Books, 1987.

Thomson, J. Oliver. *History of Ancient Geography.* Cambridge University Press, 1948.

Thorpe, Benjamin. *Northern Mythology.* Wordsworth Editions Ltd, 2001.

Tudge, Colin. *The Secret Life of Trees: How They Live and Why They Matter.* Penguin Books, 2005.

Vincent, William. *The Commerce and Navigation of the Ancients in the Indian Ocean.* Volumes I and II. Asian Educational Services, 1807.

Vischer, Hanns. *Across the Sahara.* Darf Publishers, 1910.

Walker, Christopher (Editor). *Astronomy before the Telescope.* British Museum Press, 1996.

Watts, Alan. *The Weather Handbook.* Waterline Books, 1999.

Wilkes, Kenneth, Pat Langley-Price, and Philip Ouvry. *Ocean Navigator.* Adlard Coles Nautical, 2000.

Winterburn, Emily. *The Stargazer's Guide.* Constable, 2008.

Woolnough, W. G. *Direction Finding by Sun, Moon and Stars.* Angus and Roberston Ltd, 1943.

Acknowledgments

I would like to thank the following people for sharing (and enduring) the zeal that has been necessary to take this book from an idea to reality.

My family, not least my wife, sister, brother, and father for their input and support. My agent, Sophie Hicks. Louisa Joyner, Davina Russell, Toby Clarke and all the team at Virgin Books for working so tirelessly with me on the book from its conception. Margaret Stead, Ruth Murray, Fiona Vincent, David Burch, Marvin Creamer, and Tom Peppitt for playing vital roles toward the end. The many instructors, friends, and colleagues who have, over the years, shared the risks and helped shape my passion for navigation. David Palmer for serendipity and John Haggarty of South Stoke for inspiration. I am very grateful to Matthew Lore and the team at The Experiment for publishing the book in the United States.

I would also like to thank all those who have come on my natural navigation courses—this book would not have been possible without you.

Index

About the Author

Tristan Gooley set up his natural navigation school, The Natural Navigator, after studying and practicing the art for over ten years. His passion for the subject stems from hands-on experience. He has led expeditions in five continents; climbed mountains in Europe, Africa, and Asia; sailed across oceans; and piloted small aircraft to Africa and the Arctic. He is the only living person to have both flown and sailed solo across the Atlantic. Tristan is a Fellow of both the Royal Institute of Navigation and the Royal Geographical Society and is the Vice Chairman of Trailfinders. He lives with his wife and two sons in West Sussex.